Work Concepts for the Future

Managing Alternative Work Arrangements

by

Patricia Schiff Estess

Crisp Publications, Inc.
Menlo Park, CA

Work Concepts for the Future

Patricia Schiff Estess

Credits
Managing Editor: Kathleen Barcos
Editor: Janis Paris
Designer: ExecuStaff
Typesetting: ExecuStaff
Cover Design: London Road Design

Library of Congress Catalog Card Number 95-71409
Estess, Patricia Schiff
Work Concepts for the Future
ISBN 1-56052-387-5

Contents

Preface

Think back. In the years you've been employed, have you ever known anyone who has

- Worked from home on occasion because that's where he or she could think and plan most effectively?

- Worked four 10-hour days and stayed home the fifth day to tend to the needs of an elderly parent?

- Worked part-time for a few years so that she (usually) could be home with the young ones during their formative years?

- Opened the office at 7:30 a.m. so that he could leave at 3:30 p.m. to get in a few hours of study before he went to his late-afternoon college classes?

Most probably you've known some of these folks. You might have been one yourself. The difference between the "then" flexible schedulers and the "now" flexible schedulers is essentially one of visibility. Then the arrangements were informal, exclusive, outside of formal corporate or organizational policy, and perhaps even hush-hush. Now, because of the times, technology, regulations, and the needs of the workforce, organizations are seeing these flexible arrangements as central, not tangential, to their bottom lines. Now they're talking openly about them, many chiseling formal, written policies on alternative work scheduling into their corporate missions.

Even without a detailed cost-benefit analysis, alternative work arrangements that provide greater flexibility in the workplace and the hours people work have gone on for decades. Organizations know it's smart business to keep good employees by accommodating schedules as much as possible.

If ever a win-win benefit existed, alternative work arrangements is it.

Being able to adjust your work schedule

- Allows you to weave home and family obligations more comfortably into your schedule.

- Gives you more time for personal growth (college, special classes, hobbys) and community activities.

- Eases some of the commuting strain.

- Permits you to shape your schedule so you can work at times when you are at your personal best.

- Reduces some of the stress of trying to juggle work and personal life.

Quality of life has become an important issue on the work front. As an employee and/or as a supervisor, chances are it's important to you as well. People in every department of your organization are concerned about their ability to balance their work and personal lives. They're overwhelmed and overworked, a fact that's borne out on their real or imaginary "time cards" as well as in their heads. Consider this: Americans average more than 45 hours a week on job-related activities. Yet, even if people love going to work and are challenged by their jobs, they have additional responsibilities—to themselves and others—and other activities they want to pursue—from working out at the gym to volunteering at a local school or coaching a Little League team. Even people in their 20s with no immediate family responsibilities are thinking about the work-life balance. In a 1994 poll conducted by *Fortune Magazine,* those in their 20s were found to be working an average of 45 hours a week. They said they would be willing to cut back to 39 hours—with a pay cut to match. And when the newly careered adults were asked which is more important to them, their personal lives or their careers, the former won hands down—64 to 36 percent. Twentysomething adults are telling us that the directive to "get a life" is alive and well.

The problem is that personal matters cannot always be wrapped neatly around a fulltime Monday through Friday 9-to-5 arrangement.

Chapter 1

Alternative Work Schedules: Why Now?

If You Had Your Choice

Take a moment to think about how you would arrange your working schedule right now if you had a choice.

- *Would you want to work from home a few times a week?*

- *Compress your work week into four days? Three and a half days?*

- *Share your job with someone else, thus working halftime instead of a full week?*

- *Change your hours so that you started earlier and left earlier? Started later and worked later?*

If you want to continue your schedule as it is, do you ever foresee a time when you might want a different work schedule?

When? _____

What might that be? _____

_____

_____

Flexible Scheduling at Different Times in Life

It is during transitional times in one's lifetime that the need for time flexibility becomes most compelling. Some of these times of transition are

New marriage

Becoming a parent

Divorce and single parenting

Death of spouse, child, or close relative

Assuming responsibility for elderly relative

Impending retirement

Almost all new parents, for example, grapple with how they are going to create more time to bond, care for, and play with their babies. And they have every reason to be concerned. Between 1969 and 1989 parents increased their total workloads—both inside and outside the home—by more than three weeks per year. Younger parents bore the brunt of these changes; moms between the ages of 18 and 39 toiled an additional 241 hours per year, and younger dads put in an extra 189 annually.

Parents are parents, and coming through the doors into a work environment doesn't change that. Studies indicate that a third of employees with children at home spend time while they are on the job worrying about the care of their children. Not only that, they act on their concern. Each month 35 percent of mothers with children younger than 12 have a sick child and 51 percent of them miss work to care for the child.

Women returning from maternity leave often welcome a slow transition back to a full work week, perhaps starting with three days for the first two months, adding a fourth day during the next two months, and when the baby is six months old, coming back fulltime. And in many families, the desire to be home with school-aged children is so strong that parents look for ways to overlap their work schedules, so that one can be home with the children in the morning to get them ready for school and the other can be home when the children come back at the end of the day.

When relatives become elderly, working people (most frequently women) are pressed to provide them with some care. One-quarter of the working-age population describes itself as responsible for an elder. These people spend an average of between 10 and 12 hours a week at the task, and 30 percent of these provide assistance for two or more older people. Even if elderly parents don't live with their adult children (and most don't), children are expected to help their parents get needed services. Time is drawn from an already crammed day to call nursing services, investigate alternative living arrangements, do some of the relative's household chores (or locate and hire someone else to do them) and on and on. And we can expect eldercare responsibilities to increase dramatically over the next few years as the leading edge of the Baby Boom generation moves into its 50s—the peak life stage for elder caregiving.

Consider this amazing statistic: The average woman spends 17 years caring for children and 18 years caring for an aging relative. In between and simultaneously, people may spend years squeezed by responsibility to both generations.

Not for Mothers Only

Although driven by women's entrance into the labor market, the need for flexible scheduling extends to more people than just mothers. Everyone benefits—dads, couples without children, and singles.

Alternative work schedules for times of planned transitions are easier to foresee and adjust to than out-of-the-blue crisis times. Often when an emergency occurs, the employee wants or needs to continue working fulltime for the income, for the diversion the work brings, or for future career growth. But sometimes, for example, in the case of an employee whose child is getting chemotherapy treatment, that employee also wants to be with the child on the days he is getting the treatment. Will the employee take chunks of unpaid leave under the Family and Medical Leave Act or can an alternative schedule be arranged that would allow the employee to accomplish his or her work tasks without losing any pay and still be at the child's side?

From an employee's point of view, working on a schedule that meets personal and job needs is ideal. And people are doing just that. There are whole new breeds of people in the workforce, and these three types described in *Breaking Out of 9 to 5* by Maria Laqueur and Donna Dickinson are turning to flexible arrangements to fulfill dreams:

Downshifters	Those people who jump off the fast track to reduce stress and strike a balance between work and personal interests.
Plateauers	Those who intentionally put their careers on hold by turning down promotions in favor of devoting time and energy to other activities.
Portfolio people	Those who develop an array or portfolio of skills that allow them to move easily among a variety of assignments or jobs.

From the Employer's Point of View

Alternative work scheduling makes good business sense. It accomplishes the following:

- Morale increases when employees know the company is sensitive to their precarious work-life balancing act. Their commitment to the organization increases.

- The company can stretch the number of hours during the day in which it does business. When people work flexible hours or compressed workweeks, daily coverage is extended and more people can be available when intense coverage is needed. The additional coverage is especially important in today's global economy when more and more business is done with people and companies in different time zones.

- A company has an edge when trying to recruit and retain talented employees—especially in a tight job market or when it is competing for workers with special skills.

- Stress-related illness drops—which means less absenteeism and lower insurance premiums. (A study done of Johnson & Johnson employees found that workers using flexible time and family-leave policies were absent 50 percent less than the workforce as a whole!) Lateness also drops significantly.

- Companies and organizations find it easier to comply with government regulations, such as the Clean Air Act and the Americans with Disabilities Act, because employees are coming into the office at off-hours or are able to work from home, thus not congesting traffic during peak hours.

- Employee productivity improves.

Interestingly, studies indicate that the company benefits even more than employees from flexible arrangements. The reduction of tardiness, improvements in attitude, reduction of absenteeism, and increased recruiting advantages are more significant to the company than the role of alternative scheduling is in solving work-family conflict.

From the Manager's Point of View

In a time when organizations are restructuring, downsizing, and up-grading, managers are being squeezed out. Those with the greatest skills in making work flow effortlessly and in mentoring, coaching, and motivating people will be most successful in the workplaces of the year 2000 and beyond. So a company policy that embraces alternative work arrangements and provides management training for implementing these arrangements works to a manager's benefit by:

- Using and honing the mentoring, coaching, and motivating skills so necessary for the future.

- Providing managers with the opportunity to balance their own work and personal lives.

As ideal as the option for flexible scheduling seems to individuals and the organization, as a manager, you are responsible for making it work. Clearly, you face difficult challenges.

1. You have to make the final determination as to whether a job is appropriate for an alternative schedule, how it meshes with your department's needs, and whether the person requesting flexible arrangements meets your criteria (or the company's policy standards).

2. You have to maintain a cooperative team spirit among two different groups—those on regular schedules and those on flexible schedules.

3. You have to make certain client service needs continue to be met.

4. You have to figure out how to measure and evaluate the performances of people working on alternative work arrangements.

5. You have to stay in touch with, provide direction for, and communicate the company culture and goals to employees you might not see frequently.

6. In addition to procedural barriers and difficulties, you have to confront your own attitude and the overt or covert resistance of others to flexible work arrangements.

Most Frequently Used Alternative Work Arrangements

In this book, we will focus on the most currently used alternative work arrangements—flextime, flexplace or telecommuting, compressed work-weeks, part-time, job sharing, and phased return and retirement. Usage among these is growing in geometric proportions. Many of these have a variety of forms; many can be used in combination with others.

Flextime

Schedules that permit employees to choose their starting and quitting times within limits set by management. The flexible periods usually are at either end of a designated core time.

Compressed Workweeks

A standard workweek compressed into fewer than five days. Arrangements most frequently used: (A) Four 10-hour days, (B) Three 12-hour days, (C) One two-week pay period with five 8-hour days in the first week and four 10-hour days plus a free day in the second week.

Flexplace or Telecommuting

Work at home or at satellite offices on a regular basis. Most telecommuting arrangements are less than five days a week. Employees use available technology—computer, FAX, telephone—to stay connected to the office.

Regular Part-Time

Less than fulltime work by employees on a company's regular payroll. Ideally this option offers the same job security and a pro-rata share of the benefits available to fulltime workers.

Job-Sharing

Two people assume the responsibilities of one fulltime job. Salary and benefits are prorated. Unlike two people doing part-time work, job sharing requires a close team approach to job responsibilities and allows for more continuity because partners can trade time or fill in for each other.

Voluntary Reduced Work Time

Often initiated by an employer as a cost-saving measure, this is a voluntary time/income trade-off that allows employees to reduce time and income (and take a prorated cut in benefits). It is usually used for a short period of time and guarantees employees a return to fulltime status.

Work Sharing

Don't be confused by the name; employees do not share the work in the sense of sharing the same job. Instead, this arrangement is often used as an alternative to layoffs. It is an involuntary arrangement whereby all or part of an organization's workforce temporarily reduces hours and salary, and in some instances receive partial unemployment payments.

Phased Retirement

Options for older workers to reduce their hours for a period of time prior to retirement. Phased retirement programs generally define a timeline to retirement.

Phased Return

Options to women on maternity leave, men on paternity leave, or those who have been out on disability. Phased return programs generally define a timeline for returning.

Leaves and Sabbaticals

Authorized periods of time away from work. Paid or unpaid leaves can be used for a variety of reasons, including community service, education, travel, recovery from illness or accident, or caring for dependent family members.

Chapter 2

Overcoming Barriers
to
Flexible Scheduling

A 9-to-5 mindset is an attitude and a habit—not sacred organizational gospel. And attitudes (both your own and others) are hard to shake and harder to overcome than policy or program obstacles. That's why even the most forward-thinking companies find themselves stymied when they try to introduce alternative work arrangements.

If you didn't realize why implementing alternative work scheduling is important to the company, you (as a person and as a manager) wouldn't be reading this book.

Still, while your intellect says "it makes sense," your gut may be resisting. That is why it's best to reflect on your own attitude about when and where work can be accomplished so you can better deal with your own biases.

The following self-quiz will help. No right or wrong answers exist. But some beliefs stand in the way of effectively implementing and managing people on alternative work arrangements. We'll address those after you take the quiz.

How Do I Really *Feel* About Flexible Scheduling?

Check what you feel generally applies as true or false.

	True	False
FROM MY PERSONAL PERSPECTIVE		
People who work on alternative schedules are mainly women.	☐	☐
If women want careers, they should not have children.	☐	☐
People have to handle their personal problems before or after work, not during it.	☐	☐
I didn't have access to this flexibility when I needed it, why should others?	☐	☐
FROM MY MANAGERIAL PERSPECTIVE		
People expect to work a 9-to-5 schedule. They flounder and are uncomfortable with anything different.	☐	☐
People abuse the privileges associated with alternative scheduling.	☐	☐
When people are not at their desks or when they're coming and going at different times, work is not getting done.	☐	☐
People who work at home don't have critical jobs.	☐	☐
If people were really committed to this company, they wouldn't jeopardize their jobs by asking for an alternative work schedule.	☐	☐

	True	False
Someone working a flexible schedule isn't interested in career advancement.	☐	☐
If one person goes on an alternative work schedule, everyone is going to want it.	☐	☐
This isn't going to work in my department, so why even try.	☐	☐
If I can't see someone I'm supervising, I'll lose control over the situation.	☐	☐

If you've answered "generally true" to many of these statements, you may find yourself unconsciously sabotaging an employee's flexible scheduling (or turning down requests) because your attitudes are working against the arrangement.

The Changing Workforce

The face of the workforce has been changing for quite a while. Perhaps the following will help you see things in a different light.

More women than ever are actively working outside the home. By the turn of the century it is expected that more than 50 percent of all employees in the United States will be women and 75 percent of all women between the ages 45 and 60 will be working.

Women are having children and working. Mothers with preschool children make up the fastest-growing segment of the labor force. Working women of childbearing years made up 80 percent of all working women in 1991, and the vast majority—anywhere from 75 to 93 percent—will become pregnant at some point during their work life. Most will return to work before their child's first birthday.

For most women, their income is essential not only to their own well-being but to that of their families (so the question of whether they *should* work becomes moot).

Alternative scheduling is not just for mothers. It is a work option that must be available to everyone (within certain parameters)—because motherhood isn't life's only responsibility. So is fatherhood. So is caring for a sick or ailing spouse or parent. So is caring for oneself. And since a person's responsibilities change during a lifetime, the need for alternative work schedules fluctuates.

And if your response is still a "what about me?" reaction . . . if an altered work schedule wasn't available to you as you were coming up through the ranks, don't you wish it had been? Wouldn't it have made your life easier? Isn't there a possibility that there will be a time in your life when you foresee the need or desire for a flexible schedule?

Confronting Your Fears

You probably won't be surprised to know that most people *do* feel most comfortable with a 9-to-5 job at a work site—for most of their working lives. But there are times when they want, or need, to alter their schedules.

Everyone Will Want to Do It!

Don't be concerned that an alternative work arrangement is contagious. Just because one person feels the need to switch a schedule, this doesn't mean the whole department will come down with "flexibilitis." Even in the most supportive corporate cultures, only about 10 percent of the workforce will be interested in flexibility at any given time.

By its very definition, flexible scheduling isn't a lifetime commitment. Its principal use in the workplace is to meet a short-term need for either the employee or the employer.

What About Abuse?

Nor is an alternative work arrangement necessarily dangerous. Abuse occurs when people are working on flexible schedules probably less frequently than when they're working on a regular schedule. We all know about the not-so-subtle ploys of on-site employees who goof off. They look industrious while paying household bills or wait until the manager leaves for a meeting and then make personal phone calls. Some newly devised ploys are bound to happen when people are on flexible schedules.

But mainly, people on alternative work schedules are more, rather than less, productive. You don't need psychology 101 to understand why. When a company is responsive to a person's personal needs, that person is more likely to be appreciative than abusive. Appreciation is expressed in the form of increased productivity, higher morale, greater commitment, and more flexibility on the employee's part (willingness to come in on an off-hour for a special meeting, for example). Employees don't want to sacrifice career advancement or raises because they're on alternative schedules. Nor should they, if they're being as productive or more productive than they were on traditional work schedules.

As a Manager of Others on Flexible Work Arrangements

The fear of most managers is that they won't be able to properly supervise people on alternative work arrangements. And to some extent that fear is justified—especially if they think of management as face-to-face supervision and doing things the way they have always done them. It is true that different management skills are necessary when employees are working on flexible schedules, and we'll be addressing those new skills and how to acquire them throughout the book. In the meantime, remember that objectives can be set and met, regardless of who's on what work schedule.

It's impossible to foresee all the challenges you'll face when you institute an alternative work arrangement, not because they're overwhelming but because you're still in unchartered waters and because each case is different. Expect to pilot any program or any individual flexible schedule for at least three months, and to make ongoing modifications even when a program is well underway.

Senior Management Support

Few in senior management can refute the evidence that gives a "two-thumbs up" for alternative work arrangements. Most embrace the concept—at least intellectually.

But making intrinsic changes in the way business is conducted doesn't happen overnight. It is an ongoing process—not likely to come to fruition with a one-time introduction, even if that introduction is accompanied by fanfare. If a genuine commitment to alternative work arrangements is made, senior management will continuously communicate its enthusiasm and support to all levels—and specifically to supervisors. Here's what you should expect.

1. **A clear and ongoing explanation as to why alternative work arrangements are important to the organization and how they meet business needs.** This should appear in written form in the annual report, mission statement, in-house publications, and in interviews on the subject by seniors in the consumer and trade press. And it should be reiterated often in meetings and interoffice communication.

2. **An explanation of what specific changes in supervisors' behavior will be required.** Will supervisors be asked to redesign work and jobs and come up with creative ways to satisfy customer needs in nontraditional ways?

3. **Explicit company support and help with implementing the changes.** Management training should be forthcoming. The company should be prepared to make changes in the scope of benefits offered to part-time employees. Will adjustments in head-count procedures be made?

4. **Acknowledgment that supervisors have successfully implemented flexible scheduling in their units, departments, or divisions.** Performance reviews should be changed to include "managing flexibility." Systems should be in place to survey customers on how the new scheduling affects service to them. The way your productivity is evaluated might be different. If you don't have this ongoing reinforcement, you, as a manager, might waffle in your own commitment because you're uncertain how introducing alternative work arrangements will affect your standing within the company.

The Subtle and Not-So Subtle Support

You know you have a clear-cut mandate from management when certain policies and strategies are in place:

▶ **A written policy on alternative working scheduling.** Having a written policy, whether in a special work-family or work-life handbook or as part of the regular benefits handbook, signifies and solidifies commitment—to the principle, not to the granting of every request for an alternative work schedule. When it comes to written policy, general is better than specific. A few samples of general written policy are presented in this section.

Sample Policy from a Publishing Company

Alternative work schedules are options that can be implemented to accommodate employee needs and retain a talented workforce. Flexible work arrangements may be used by management where business needs allow and where we can maintain the quality and productivity of our organization. Successful alternative work schedules require open communication between managers and employees in developing solutions to work and family conflicts.

Criteria of Eligibility: The individual's performance rating must be satisfactory, and the responsibilities of the job must be conducive to job flexibility. In the case involving recruitment of an individual, the job responsibilities must allow for flexible scheduling.

Requirements: The employee in conjunction with the manager must submit a written proposal for the alternative work arrangements. Each request for a flexible work arrangement will be evaluated individually by senior management and Human Resources according to job requirements and individual circumstances. Assistance can be provided by the Human Resource Department.

Sample Policy from a Bank

The need for an adjustment in your work schedule because of family responsibilities can arise at any time in your career. If you have special family-care needs, you may pursue the possibility of an alternative work arrangement, with your manager's approval. Managers may take prior performance, job requirements, departmental staffing and the expected duration of the alternative work arrangement into account in determining whether an alternative arrangement is appropriate. Typical alternative work arrangement options include gradual return to work after parental leave, part-time schedules, job-sharing and working an adjusted daily schedule. For more information about alternative work arrangement options, please contact your employee relations representative or [name and phone number of work-life coordinator].

Note that in these sample policies, alternative work scheduling is limited to those with work and family conflicts. This is not true in all companies. Some make the alternative scheduling available to anyone—as long as the nature of the job duties allow for it, work performance record is high, and the manager is able to work out the arrangement.

> *From Hal Lancaster's* **Wall Street Journal** *column on "Managing Your Career" comes this somewhat tongue-in-cheek suggestion for a generic corporate flexibility policy that's open to everybody:*
>
> *All forms of flexible scheduling are welcomed at this company as long as the work gets done efficiently. Managers and team leaders can negotiate with employees any such arrangement that meets that requirement without bureaucratic interference from all of us deep-thinking policy makers on the top floor. We'll review these decisions in frequent performance reviews and take whatever action is necessary to fix the ones that don't work.*

▶ **Policies and programs are frequently communicated.** This should occur both within the company and to the outside world. When this happens, the company's in-house publication is brimming with success stories of people working on alternative arrangements or managers open to flexible scheduling, the CEO talks about it with and to other CEOs, testimonials are welcomed from others in the company who have successfully incorporated the concept, and everyone within the company is aware that someone (usually someone in the human resources department) has been appointed to answer the nuts and bolts questions about policies and guidelines.

▶ **Flexible work arrangements are operating at senior management levels.** This can apply to offices of the CEO and other senior managers. If, for example, the senior vice president has two assistants sharing one job—one working in the mornings and the other in the afternoons—that sends a signal to other managers that such an arrangement is doable and sanctioned.

► **People working flexible arrangements are acknowledged as valuable.** They are promoted, given appropriate raises, and recognized for their contributions. This reinforces the fact that people on alternative work schedules are committed, productive, and valuable to the company. It makes employees less reticent to suggest an alternative work arrangement at times when it is important to them.

► **Employees are not penalized financially.** Benefits and salary structures for those on flexible schedules are fair and in line with those people who work the more standard way. Benefits must be prorated for people working on reduced work schedules, not eliminated.

► **Guidelines are provided to management.** Training programs are established for people who are (or will be) managing others on alternative work schedules. A company's dollar commitment to training is a signal to managers that the firm is serious about the policy. Written guidelines are provided but not so formal that they limit the manager's creativity.

► **Managers are empowered to make individual work arrangements.** They should also be rewarded for being creative. That reward comes in the form of more favorable performance reviews (where they are evaluated on their ability to manage their resources, develop employees, and foster teamwork) which ultimately translates into an increase in salary or position.

Strategies for Enhancing Support

If you get the feeling that there's a lot of talk about alternative work arrangements, but little conviction (because the mandates don't seem to be there), you might want to consider beefing up senior managers' commitment by engaging in a number of the following strategies:

CATHY © 1994 Cathy Guisewite. Reprinted with permission of UNIVERSAL PRESS SYNDICATE. All rights reserved.

- Find a member of the senior management team who will act as a champion for alternative work arrangements.

- Get a number of other managers from different departments and divisions involved in the process of implementing flexible arrangements.

- Regularly share studies and supporting information for flexible scheduling reported in newspapers and magazines.

- Find out what competitors are doing and share that information with senior management.

- Connect alternative work arrangements to a business strategy or goal.

- Talk about a vision while piloting alternative work arrangements and implementing them on an incremental basis.

- Provide management with feedback on the challenges you face and how you are overcoming them. Share your successes.

Chapter 3

Flexibility: New Concepts for Managers and Employees

For some people a job has never been something you do from 9 to 5. Those who work "shifts" (nurses, security guards, police officers, fire fighters) know that someone with similar skills needs to be on the job around the clock, so they work in the early morning and during the day, in the late afternoon and into the evening, or throughout the night.

Those who service populations at nontraditional hours (sanitation workers who collect garbage at night, dinner chefs, nightclub owners, and so on) often have to rearrange their lives around their work schedules.

Many creative people (such as writers, artists, computer programmers, etc.) who aren't tied to any schedule except meeting a deadline set their own hours and work whenever their productivity and creative juices are at their highest.

Still, a perception persists in the business world that a "job" is something you do from 9 to 5 and that it is defined in number of hours worked. The problem is that these eight-hour efforts no longer serve as the building blocks of an organization's structure.

Redefining What a Job Is

If alternative work arrangements are going to benefit the company, managers must think of most jobs in terms of performance and tasks accomplished, not time on the job or time under the watchful eye of a supervisor.

A Job's Component Parts

Before a supervisor can respond with a, "Yes" or a "No" to an employee's request for a flexible work arrangement, he or she has to understand the component parts of the person's job and what priority each of those parts has.

Once that's understood, it's easier to see what parts can be done at home or early in the morning before anyone else is in the office. For example, by asking the following questions, you can begin identifying the components of any job.

- When is the best time to do each of the tasks that make up the job?

- Where can each be done?

- Who does this person have to work with to accomplish one or more of the tasks?

- How can this person communicate with the people he or she needs to communicate with?

- What deadlines are attached to each task?

- What is the objective of each task?

Example: Operations Manager

Now, let's break down the job of an operations manager in a 25-person office in a nonprofit organization.

Component: *Security*

> **Task:** *Develop office procedures at reception desk to ensure safety.*
>
> **When is best time to do it?** *Anytime new receptionist is hired or when new problem develops.*
>
> **Where can it be done?** *Plan can be done anywhere; implementation must be done in office.*
>
> **Who does it involve?** *Receptionist, executive director, entire office staff.*
>
> **How can we communicate?** *Face to face initially.*
>
> **Deadline?** *Immediately, then as needed.*

Component: *Supplies*

> **Task:** *Procure adequate office supplies at best prices.*
>
> **When is best time to do it?** *Anytime.*
>
> **Where can it be done?** *On-site inspection of supplies necessary once a month. Otherwise, negotiating price/quality and follow-up reports can be done anywhere.*
>
> **Who does it involve?** *Entire staff needs to provide feedback.*
>
> **How can we communicate?** *Memos, meetings, e-mail, bulletin boards.*
>
> **Deadline?** *Supplies ordered on 25th of month; emergency supplies ordered whenever necessary.*

Component: *Printing*

> **Task:** *See that the cost and process of printing monthly newsletter is efficient.*

When is best time to do it? *Newsletter goes to printer on 15th of each month. Process takes 10 days, during which time, printer and operations manager are in daily communication on production.*

Where can it be done? *Communication most easily done from office; could be done from home.*

Who does it involve? *Printer, editor, and operations manager.*

How can we communicate? *Fax, phone, and Federal Express.*

Deadline? *Must be finished and in the mail on the 25th of each month.*

Component: *Personnel*

Task: *Oversee the orientation of new hires.*

When is best time to do it? *Discuss benefits with person prior to his/her coming on board. Spend two hours on first day discussing company procedures and orienting new employee to physical layout and benefit procedures.*

Where can it be done? *In office.*

Who does it involve? *New employees.*

How can we communicate? *Face to face.*

Deadline? *Week before and on day new person begins job.*

Component: *Benefits*

Task: *Design a new health benefit plan to lower costs to company and increase coverage for employees.*

When is best time to do it? *Anytime.*

Where can it be done? *From anywhere. Once employee survey is completed, results and follow-up research is probably best done out of the office (fewer interruptions).*

Who does it involve? *Initially all employees. Thereafter, periodic meetings with executive director.*

How can we communicate? *With executive director: face to face, e-mail, fax, phone, memo.*

Deadline? *September 30.*

Exercise: Your Own Job

Now take your own job and break it down into its component parts. In phrasing the task, be sure to include the goals of each component.

Component: _____

  Task: _____

  When is best time to do it? _____

  Where can it be done? _____

  Who does it involve? _____

  How can we communicate? _____

  Deadline? _____

Component: _____

  Task: _____

  When is best time to do it? _____

  Where can it be done? _____

  Who does it involve? _____

  How can we communicate? _____

  Deadline? _____

Component: _____

  Task: _____

  When is best time to do it? _____

  Where can it be done? _____

  Who does it involve? _____

  How can we communicate? _____

  Deadline? _____

Component: _____

   Task: _____

   When is best time to do it? _____

   Where can it be done? _____

   Who does it involve? _____

   How can we communicate? _____

   Deadline? _____

Component: _____

   Task: _____

   When is best time to do it? _____

   Where can it be done? _____

   Who does it involve? _____

   How can we communicate? _____

   Deadline? _____

Applying Flexibility to the Components of Your Job

Going back to the "If I Had My Choice" exercise in Chapter 1, review the areas in which you would like to achieve some flexibility in your work schedule. Now take the component parts of your job and see if you can create a schedule for yourself that would allow you to have your choice at the same time you're accomplishing all that you have to accomplish (perhaps even more productively than you are doing these now).

Ask yourself a few more questions:

1. Are any of the tasks you're doing superfluous?

2. Could you be doing any of these tasks differently so that they could be done more quickly or more productively?

3. Should any tasks be added to your list because they need to be done (and aren't getting done now) or because you could do them more effectively, more easily, or more conveniently than someone else?

4. Could any of the tasks be done more conveniently, more easily, or more effectively by another person?

5. What is the priority of all these tasks?

As you divide a job into its component tasks and determine whether or not these tasks are appropriately designed and assigned, you're engaging in a creative exercise. You are reshaping a job from work that's traditionally measured in hours to work that's redesigned into tasks accomplishing desired goals. This exercise is important for anyone considering an alternative work arrangement. (Actually it's useful for *all* employees, even those on regular schedules.)

Helping Employees Become More Self-Directed

All evidence points to more productivity and employee commitment when people have greater control over their jobs. So when an employee approaches you with idea for redesigning his or her job, think of it as a plus rather than an inconvenience.

And it will be . . . because people on flexible arrangements become independent and self-directed if the arrangement works well.

An Employee's Proposal

Before requesting an alternative work arrangement, an employee needs to have thought through a great many questions, including specifically how a particular arrangement would be best for him or her *and* best for the department and the company.

Strategically, it also makes sense for the employee to determine the best time (during a performance review, after having finished an important project, after having been congratulated by the president for outstanding work, or simply at the end of a pleasant day) and the best approach (formal or informal, at first) for making such a request. (But certainly you, the manager, shouldn't hear about it through the grapevine first.)

After an initial discussion, the responsibility for moving the idea along belongs to the employee. You have a right to expect a formal proposal from him or her. It's important for many reasons:

- It helps an employee organize his or her thoughts.

- It spells out specifics that can be agreed upon (or negotiated).

- It allows you to address potential problem areas and offer possible solutions.

- It provides you with a written document that you can present to senior management if you need to justify your decision whether or not to grant the flexible arrangement.

- It serves as the basis of an understanding between you and the employee.

What to Include on a Proposal

Naturally every proposal will be different, but most should include the following (and you should share this with any employee who is about to draft a request).

1. What the proposed work schedule is (number of hours per day and per week; place or places work will be accomplished; how long the employee expects to use this arrangement).

2. What the advantages to the company and to the department are. Any of these might be applicable: To retain an experienced and skillful employee; reduce employee burnout, thereby increasing enthusiasm and productivity; expand departmental coverage; or experience less employee lateness or absenteeism.

3. What, if any, job redesign will be necessary? Will all tasks now done be able to be accomplished? Is there a better way of redesigning the job?

4. How the "availability" issues will be dealt with. If there is less face-to-face contact, how will the person (1) attend meetings, (2) stay in touch with others in the department and you, (3) attend to client/customer needs, and (4) handle emergency situations?

5. What impact the flexible schedule would have on salary and benefits. Generally if a work schedule is reduced, pay and benefits are prorated. The benefits issue is complex and depends upon company policy and applicable state laws.

6. Supporting information that lets you know how this arrangement has worked in another company or another department. Adding newspaper clips on the subject or copies of reports on the pros and cons of the proposed arrangement shows you that the employee has done some research on the subject.

An Employee's Responsibility for Making It Work

Alternative work arrangements, almost by definition, mean that employees have more responsibility for designing their jobs and accomplishing their tasks. They become less like job holders and more like job owners.

As such, they play an active part in making their alternative schedules succeed—for themselves, their coworkers, you, and the company. It is their responsibility to meet the goals and expectations you both have agreed upon.

Here's what else you can reasonably expect from people on alternative work arrangements. First, they should be flexible and accommodating to unforeseen changes whenever possible (such as returning phone calls to customers or attending an urgent staff meeting on the day of the compressed workweek that they are not working).

Second, they must have a communications plan. They should make known their schedules and how they will communicate with everyone who needs that information. They should set up a system for handling calls "including a scripted line" for a receptionist. And, finally, they must stay in touch with colleagues and solicit feedback from them as to how the arrangement is working.

How the Manager's Role Might Change

With all the independence afforded employees on alternative work arrangements, one might wonder if a manager doesn't risk losing control of his or her staff.

If by control we mean rule or command—then, yes, managers do lose control under this arrangement.

But if control is defined as guide, influence, and oversight—then, no, control may even be increased. (And, as we said earlier, these are the defining management characteristics of the future.) Managing employees on flexible schedules requires increased evaluating, mentoring, organizational, monitoring, and communication skills.

Will the Arrangement Be Good for the Company?

In most cases, a manager makes the first and final evaluation on whether a job has flex potential. As a manager, you have to ask yourself how the arrangement would affect the company and your particular sphere or department.

Ask yourself:

- What advantages are there to the company that will justify this plan?

- How will staffing and workflow requirements be affected? Will peak periods be covered sufficiently?

- What impact will the new schedule have on the employee's job responsibilities? Can any negative impact be defused? Can we capitalize on the positive impact?

- What impact will this schedule have on customer/client service? If negative, can it be countermanded?

Will the Arrangement Be Good for Your Department?

If a work arrangement increases your department's productivity or bottom line, it will reflect on your own skills as a manager. Be aware, however, that if alternative work scheduling is new to your department, you may have to lay some groundwork before you agree to an employee's flexible scheduling request. In addition to the obvious questions to ask yourself, such as how many hours are required to do the job and are there limitations on where the job can be done, consider what consequences the arrangement will have on you and members of your department.

Ask yourself:

- Is the person making the request performing well now? If not, is that because of a scheduling problem that an alternative arrangement might help? Does the company have a policy against granting flexible arrangements to poor performers? (Many do.)

- Is the person making the request an untitled leader among his or her peers? If so, will the alternative schedule dissolve the group's cohesiveness? Is so, how can that be countered?

- Has the person requesting the flexible schedule satisfied all your questions with regard to availability, communicating, and performance requirements?

- Is there a generally cooperative atmosphere in the department? What can I do to foster greater unity?

- Will alternative work arrangements be considered a perk and therefore resented by people who are working a regular schedule? If so, what can I do to overcome this?

- Will any additional pressure be put on people working regular schedules? If so, what can I do to prevent this?

- What kinds of additional training might members of my staff need to make this arrangement work more smoothly, such as cross-training or feedback training?

- Will there be a trial period and, if so, how long should it be?

- What criteria will be used to evaluate the success of the arrangement?

- Am I comfortable enough with flexible scheduling that I won't interpret a request as a sign that the employee isn't serious about his or her job—or think that he or she is willing to forego promotion or a salary increase? If I still harbor these thoughts, what can I do to rethink the subject?

- Do I have the authority to institute such a program, readjust it, and terminate it, if necessary?

No Easy Answers

As managers find themselves in a whole new management role, that of supervising people who may not be working in the office or who may not be working at times when regular staff members are around, new questions arise—questions that don't necessarily have right or wrong answers. For a manager in one company, the answer to some of these questions may be obvious. For another manager in another department— or another company—the opposite answer might be just as obvious. Deciding these questions calls many factors into play. Some are conscious elements that have to be considered; others are issues that are buried in your subconscious and not easily understood.

Some examples of *obvious* elements are the following:

- The needs of your department

- The corporate culture under which you operate

- The value of the employee to your department and your organization in general

- The morale of your department

- The stability of your job, the company, and the economy

- The public relations factor

Here are some examples of *not-so-obvious* elements:

- Your comfort level with change (which translates into your own willingness to go out on a limb)

- Your personal feelings toward the employee

- The amount of power you feel you have within the company

Keep these in mind when you tackle "No Easy Answers—No Right Answers" at the end of the following chapters.

Flexibility Is a Process—Not a Program

Unless alternative work arrangements are authorized by the company and employees have no say in how they will be working (which is, itself, an inflexible arrangement), think of these arrangements as having a certain amount of fluidity.

The Arrangement Might Not Be for Long

People often request a flexible arrangement only for a specific period of time or long enough to help them handle a particular personal situation.

Business Needs Change

While an employee's flexible schedule might have no bearing on his or her job one year, it might hinder the successful completion of the same job the next year. (Consider, for example, someone who opts to work a flextime schedule of 6:00 a.m. to 2.00 p.m. If that person's major account is in England, the schedule works well. If he or she loses the English account and picks up one from Japan, the early schedule would be a disaster.

Flexible Arrangements Need Regular Fine-Tuning

Alternative arrangements are new for most managers and most employees, so even if you have a written agreement and have discussed most of the major issues in advance of instituting any changes, you won't know where the kinks are until the arrangement begins operating. Let the employee know that your need for frequent feedback is to find ways to forestall serious problems, and not because you're planning to scratch the arrangement if hitches develop.

Establish a Trial Period

You always have the option of discontinuing the arrangement. Although a trial period of about *three months* is recommended, during which you and the employee meet frequently to monitor the possible areas of concern and figure out ways to mitigate problems, you always have the right to terminate the arrangement if there's a good reason. Among the "good" reasons: The customer isn't being properly serviced; the employee isn't meeting the goals and expectations that you've agreed upon; the arrangement is too expensive to the company; the person's absence has a detrimental effect on his or her colleagues.

Caution: Don't continue an unsatisfactory arrangement. But do all that you can to make it work before terminating it.

Chapter 4

Flextime: Win-Win at Its Best

As a practice, flextime (scheduling that permits flexible starting and quitting times within limits set by the company or the manager) has been going on for centuries—though it has mainly been confined to a small number of employees or done on a case-by-case basis.

As a policy, it's being touted in major companies and written about in the press. Still it's not as universally accepted as one might expect. It's hard to figure out why there's any resistance. If ever a benefit existed that serves the interests of both employee and employer, flextime is it.

Benefits to Employees

For employees, the advantages of flexible hours are fairly obvious.

It allows them to create a better balance between work and personal responsibilities. Life's obligations don't sandwich themselves neatly around the regular 9-to-5 work schedule. Parents with children in school, for example, want to (or have to, depending upon the children's ages) have an adult around to see the children off to school (usually somewhere between 7:00 and 8:45 a.m.) and greet them when they return home (generally from 2:00 to 6:00 p.m.). A growing number of couples are flexing their hours. One parent works an early schedule, but is home when school is out. The other gets the kids ready for school, but doesn't come home from work until early evening.

But flextime is not for parents only. Adult children with eldercare responsibilities may have to take a parent for physical therapy treatments during the day on a twice-a-week schedule. People who are going to college at night might have an hour's commute to get their Tuesday and Thursday evening classes.

Flextime allows people to work at their "personal best" times. Some people spring into action at the dawn of each day; others when the sun sets. And no matter how much coffee they pump into themselves during their "off" hours, if the time isn't right for their biological clock, they will not be particularly productive.

It also allows them time during the day to work in a somewhat uninterrupted manner, because during some of the hours that they're working, fewer colleagues and customers are around to break concentration either with phone calls, meetings, or chats. Paper and computer work go much faster. Creative thoughts have quiet time to hatch.

Benefits to the Company

For the company or organization, the advantages of flextime are just as powerful.

It improves the service available to customers. Even small firms probably have some business dealings with companies or people in other time zones. So when it's 5:00 p.m. and closing time at your office, it may be two, three, or four hours earlier at one of your customer's offices. If your office staff has gone home for the day, you might miss an important call or message. The same holds true on the other side of the day. Your employees might be sauntering in at 9:05 a.m. only to find a dozen messages on their answering machine from impatient customers who have been at work for hours (and who are now out to lunch when your employees get around to calling back). Flextime opens the window of time during which you can conduct business.

It also improves the coverage to others in the company. People in different departments often work on different schedules, so having people around early in the day and into the evening to field questions or work with others in the company can be extremely useful in maintaining the work flow.

Flextime can increase productivity. Because people appreciate the opportunity to set their own hours (within boundaries established by the company and the department), they are much more appreciative, supportive, loyal, and ultimately productive. And . . . they no longer take time off for doctor and dentist appointments! That can be done during their flextime personal hours. Flextime reduces overtime and is the most immediately appreciated of all the alternative work arrangements.

Office and facilities are more effectively used. The additional time on either side of the day means that computer networks are easier to log onto and nobody has to wait in line to use the copy machines.

An additional bonus is that it provides your company a way of meeting the Clean Air Act standards set by the federal government. Peak commuting times are flattened out so the pollution level from auto traffic will drop during these times.

A Manager's First Step

Even before an employee requests a flextime arrangement, consider these questions.

1. What's the earliest time a person can start work in the department and the latest time a person can leave? This represents the total work day in which flextime can be scheduled. Part of your decision will rest on whether there is ample security during the stretch hours.

2. What's the time period during which all employees must be at work because of peak activity? It usually is a five- or six-hour stretch in the middle of the day—but not always; each company is different.

3. What would be the advantages to the company of flextime in my department or area?

4. Will all my employees have an opportunity to participate? If not, why not? (Check company policy.)

Let's assume you now have the answers to these questions fairly well fixed in your mind, and that a person on your staff requests flextime. Now is the time to get even more specific with your questions to yourself and the employee.

Ask yourself the following:

- How will staffing and workflow requirements be affected? If you have more than one person on flextime, it's helpful to chart the flextime schedules to be certain peak periods are covered.

- What impact, if any, will the new schedule have on the employee's job responsibilities? If the employee will not be in the office at the end of the day, will someone else be able to answer her calls? Will she be able to take over a responsibility of the person covering for her at the end of the day?

- How will departmental communications be affected? If *staff meetings* are usually Tuesday mornings at 9:00 a.m., for example, what changes will have to be made to accommodate those people working from 11:00 a.m. to 7:00 p.m.?

- How will contingencies be addressed? How will *sickness* be handled? If the early bird is sick and won't be in, would he have to call you at 4 a.m.—heaven forbid—to let you know? How will *holidays* be handled? If everyone is being let off early the day before a holiday, how will that effect the early bird? The late riser?

- Since you are not going to be in the office during the total work day in which people are working flexible hours, how will you supervise someone who is in the office when you're not? Is *on-site supervision* necessary?

- Will there be a trial period? When and how will the success of the arrangement be measured? Evaluation should also take into consideration how customers, clients, and colleagues are faring under this arrangement.

Ask your employee the following:

- For instance, will the flextime be practical for your job? What happens if, say, your major customer becomes angry because he calls you in the morning and you're not in until 11:00 a.m.? Also, do you think the morning (afternoon) is the time when you're most productive? (That's more of a "think-about-it-yourself" question than one that needs an answer.)

- How will you communicate the change in schedule to all those who need to know? What will your voice mail say when you're not in the office?

- How flexible can you be, especially during the time of closing the books for the month, for example? How flexible are you on a daily basis? (Sometimes the employee will be able to be as flexible as you need him to be; other times, other obligations prevent any flexibility on either end of the allotted time frame.)

When the employee has presented you with a written proposal addressing these issues of particular concern to you and your department, then you'll be in a position to determine if a flextime schedule is possible.

As Time Goes By—The Trial Period

As simple as flextime appears at first, you might find yourself facing some challenges a few weeks or months into the arrangement. Here are some problems and possible solutions.

The Flextimer is Not Doing His or Her Share

Managing employees working a flextime $7\frac{1}{2}$- or 8-hour day is simple. Problems arise, however, when you deal with exempt employees who, in many companies, may come in as early as 8:00 a.m. and often stay till 7:30 p.m. Colleagues become even more resentful of these brutal hours if they have to pick up the slack for one who is on flextime from 7:00 a.m. to 3:30 p.m. and can't stay later on any day because of a personal responsibility later in the day.

Possible fine-tuning solutions:

- The employee takes work home so that later in the evening he or she can finish the tasks or projects.

- The employee returns to the office later in the evening to finish up (if he or she lives close enough).

- You reassess the staffing and workflow of your department. Are you expecting too much from employees? Are there more efficient ways of handling the work so that these long hours are not expected of everyone? Should you be using part-timers, seasonal employees, or temps to alleviate unsatisfactory staffing conditions?

Client or Customer Service Seems to be Suffering

Often times you'll hear this directly from the client or customer and it needs to be addressed immediately.

Possible fine-tuning solutions:

- You expand the core time when all employees must be present.

- The employee is present at times when his or her presence is most needed, either for customer/client service or for inter-company communication.

- Have two flextimers work as a team, each becoming familiar enough with the other's customers to be able to satisfactorily service them when the other is not there.

Everybody Wants the Dawn Patrol

What do you do with the overwhelming number of requests from parents, concerned about their latchkey kids being home alone, requesting an early work start?

Possible fine-tuning solutions:

- Rotate the shifts so that everyone who wants the early shift has at least some time on it.

- Consider other alternative work arrangements, such as compressed workweeks or telecommuting.

- Ask the employees who want the dawn patrol to collaborate to find a solution.

Variations on the Flextime Theme

Many companies have come up with creative solutions to today's work-life challenges.

Flexday provides nonexempt employees with flexibility *and* pay to handle family-related emergencies. At US Sprint/United Communications, for example, nonexempts may take off two or more hours on short notice, to a maximum of one regularly scheduled day a year, to deal with family issues.

Midday flex allows employees to take off additional time (up to an hour or two) during their lunch hour, if they make up the time in the same day. This generally has to be approved by the supervisor ahead of time.

Day-to-day flextime for people who have a short-term care situation, such as someone whose spouse is in the hospital recovering from open-heart surgery (and the employee wants to be at the hospital at 3:30 p.m. every day to speak to the doctor when he or she is making rounds.

Flexible holidays days (or floating rather than fixed holidays) allow people to work on holidays. At IBM and other global companies where this flexibility exists, it means the offices can stay open 365 days a year. In effect, these multinationals no longer have to close down on all standard holidays, which may be holidays in the U.S., but are not necessarily holidays in the other countries around the world.

Flextime to attend children's school activities is the law in at least 12 states—with parents given an opportunity to make up the time so no pay is docked. At Stride Rite Corporation in Massachusetts, employees can take eight hours off every school year for parent-teacher meetings, recitals, plays, and other school activities.

Flextime combined with other alternative work arrangements works well, especially for part-time workers. About 30 percent of the Quill Corporation's part-time staff is on flextime, for example. This Illinois company has even created an "inside" temporary-services department, staffed mostly by former fulltime employees who have elected flextime. They are trained in a variety of activities and are called upon as needed—and as available—to work in different departments.

?

No Easy Answers—No "Right" Answers

How would you handle these situations? Keep in mind some of the many factors to consider: the needs of your department, your corporate culture, how valuable the employee is to your organization, the morale of your department.

What Do You Think?

You don't get the data you need for a report until 2:00 p.m. and your assistant, working a flexible schedule, leaves at 3:00 p.m. You need the report on your desk at 9:00 a.m.

Do you think it's reasonable for you to expect him to stay late, so that you can approve a rough draft that evening and he can redo it, if necessary, early the next morning so your presentation can be perfect?

If your assistant has to leave at 3:00 p.m. because he has to pick up his son at nursery school, would that make a difference in your decision?

Would the fact that he is a widower factor into your decision?

Would it make a difference if the reason he has to leave is because he is in a softball league?

What Do You Think?

Your company policy is to allow parents to take off two days a year (which can be broken up into hours if they'd like) to attend their children's school events or meetings.

Would it make a difference to you if the parent were a single parent or one of a couple? If the person asking were a man rather than a woman?

Would it make a difference if a childless worker used the two days to take care of an aging parent?

How would you feel if a childless worker wanted to take off the same two days a year to play golf?

What Do You Think?

You really benefit from having a certain employee around; he's your "go to" person. (You "go to" him with problems.) He asks for a flexible schedule that would mean he'd leave at 3:30 p.m.

Do you think it's reasonable to deny the request because you wouldn't have anyone around to troubleshoot at the end of the day?

Chapter 5

The Compressed Workweek:
Achieving More
by Condensation

With a compressed workweek, employees work the full number of hours in their regularly scheduled workweek, but the hours are compressed into fewer days. Here's how it might look, depending upon the total weekly hours employees are expected to work in your department, location, or company. (Note that working through lunch is not generally considered an acceptable way of making up the additional time required each work day.)

Normal Workweek	35 hours	37½ hours	40 hours
Three-day week	11 hours, 40 minutes	12 hours, 30 minutes	13 hours, 20 minutes
Four-day week	8 hours, 45 minutes	9 hours, 22 minutes	10 hours
Nine consecutive days, tenth day off	7 hours, 45 minutes	8 hours, 20 minutes	8 hours, 45 minutes

The arrangement has definite value to employees who want a day off every week (or every other week), but still get paid a full salary. Some might use the time to rest or take long-weekend vacations. Others might use it to matriculate for a weekend undergraduate or graduate program, for volunteer activities, to catch up on household chores or simply to have more time at home. The arrangement is especially attractive to a young, single workforce with few family responsibilities—people who don't have to rush home. They are often willing to put in more hours on a daily basis in exchange for a day off.

Decoding the New Lingo

Compressed workweek programs have titles that sound like area codes:

312   *Works 12-hour shifts over three days*

410   *Works four 10-hour days*

980   *Works 80 hours over nine workdays*

Managers often take to this arrangement as quickly as employees because it provides a relatively easy, cost-effective means of solving a business problem, such as the need to extend service hours. It's an arrangement that doesn't balloon labor costs on a permanent basis.

Consider this scenario. You need to extend the customer service hours from 8 hours a day to 10, but you can't afford to pay overtime to the nonexempt employees who staff it. If you can put together a group of employees who want to work a compressed workweek, you can set up two teams of overlapping compressed work shifts. One shift would work 8 a.m. to 6 p.m. Monday through Thursday, and the other 8 a.m. to 6 p.m. Tuesday through Friday.

Overtime Issues

In most states, compensation remains the same as if the employee worked his or her regular workweek. But not in all. In California, Alaska, Nevada, and Wyoming, for example, overtime pay legislation requires nonexempt employees in those states to be paid overtime for all hours worked in excess of eight on any one day. To limit overtime exposure, *HRMagazine* reports that employers such as Bechtel (the international construction company based in California) that use a 980 system, have rearranged their workweek so that it starts at 1:00 p.m. on Friday. Employers also may be able to avoid daily overtime by having employees approve the new schedule. All employees work the same approved schedule and agree that another vote cannot be taken for a year.

Check with your human resources or legal department on any laws dictating overtime pay for nonexempt employees in your state.

Where the Concerns Lie

Much thought has been put into these issues by corporate officers, legislators, human resource experts, managers, and employees. Their major areas of concern are these: employee stamina, adequate coverage, employee inconvenience, and exempt employees who are used to working longer days.

Stamina

Some people are dynamos, so the extra daily work hours of a compressed workweek present no problem. Others are so sapped after a regular eight-hour day that they can barely make it through dinner before falling into a comatose state in front of the TV. So as enticing as it first appears to work a four-day week and have the fifth day to themselves, some employees who opt for this arrangement may become so exhausted by the end of the second or third day that after eight hours productivity seriously slips. A trial period helps in assessing whether someone can meet the rigorous daily energy demands.

Coverage

Most departments need five- or six-day-a-week client coverage, so the idea of having coverage for only four days is horrifying at first. But compressed workweeks are most frequently set up so that teams of people work overlapping shifts. For example, group A might work Monday through Thursday, group B Tuesday through Friday, and group C Wednesday through Saturday. In addition, there may be a core of people working the standard workweek. Depending upon the department's needs, overlap can be especially effective in extending hours and beefing up coverage. Managers schedule meetings during periods of overlap to ensure adequate communication. It's also important to note that the "off" day need not necessarily be a Friday or Monday. If those are days when heaviest coverage is needed, it may not be possible for an employee to select one of those as the "off" day.

Employee Inconvenience

Public transportation and child care services, for the most part, are still set up to accommodate a 9-to-5, five-day a week schedule. So employees working from 9:00 a.m. to 7:00 p.m. four days a week, might find themselves square pegs in a round-hole society. They may have to wait an extra half an hour in the evening for a bus that's operating on a nonrush hour schedule. Or they may find that the day-care center closes at 7:00 p.m. and they have to make additional (and inconvenient) arrangements for pick-up and additional babysitting. Or their babysitter might have a family of her own to whom she has to go home. If enough employees work in a compressed workweek, often the local transit company will put on an extra bus. Or a transit pool operated by employees or the company can be set up. Employees with child-care concerns often ask neighbors and family for help during the extended hours and then swap some time during their free day with the people who have done them favors.

Exempt Employees

Compressed workweeks are least useful when the workforce is mainly an exempt staff already working many more hours weekly than the traditional 9 to 5. People cramming to complete their job responsibilities in 50 or more hours a week can't possible effectively squeeze their responsibilities into four days. Although a frenetic work pace often results in exhaustion followed by burnout, the deteriorating process will only be speeded up by a compressed workweek. (Unfortunately, over-work is a growing trend and one that companies must re-examine. It raises questions about efficiency, realistic goals, quality of product and service, and more.)

$\backsim$

The Nitty-Gritties of Vacations, Sick Days, and Holidays

To unsnarl the inherent confusion in calculating how many vacation and sick days an employee on a compressed workweek is entitled to, think of the week in terms of hours. If, for example, an employee working a four-day, 10-hour workweek is eligible to receive two weeks vacation, he or she would have eight vacation days (40 hours a week × 2 = 80 hours) which, when added to the two "off" days, would tally up to two weeks of time off.

Sick "days" now become sick "hours." If an employee working the standard 40-hour week is allowed 10 sick days a year, for example, that translates into 80 hours. An employee working a compressed work week is therefore eligible for 8 whole days of sick leave—not 10.

What happens to holidays? Realizing that a larger percentage of our holidays fall on Monday than on any other day of the week, most companies require that employees working a compressed workweek modify their schedules during holiday weeks so that employees are working regular schedules (8 hours a day, for example, instead of 10) and take off the holiday.

As many as possible of the details of compressed workweeks need to be figured out before instituting this arrangement to make sure of effective coverage, fair benefit compensation, and good communication.

Trying It Out in Summer

Many companies have their first (and in some cases, only) exposure to a compressed workweek when they go on "summer hours." That's when many compress their normal five-day workweek into $4\frac{1}{2}$ days and employees leave at 1:00 p.m. on Friday for a slightly extended weekend. (A hybrid arrangement of that is when employees alternate the Fridays they're in the office—in essence, having two shifts working 980s. Most people prefer this arrangement to going in on Friday until 1:00 p.m., because it allows them two Fridays a month free for a three-day weekend.)

?

No Easy Answers—No Right Answers

How would you handle these situations? Keep in mind some of the many factors to consider: the needs of your department, your corporate culture, how valuable the employee is to your organization, the morale of your department.

What Do You Think?

You schedule department meetings for Wednesday morning because that's when everybody is there—except for one key employee who's on a compressed workweek. Any other time or day would mean that at least four people would be unable to attend.

How would you respond when the person on the compressed workweek asks you to change the meeting day?

What Do You Think?

You have a choice of promoting one of two employees to a senior management position. Both are qualified and deserving of it. One works a regular schedule; the other works a compressed workweek and her personal circumstances don't allow her to change the arrangement.

Will the compressed workweek be a factor in your final decision?

Chapter 6

Telecommuting: The Rage of the High-Tech Era

At first glance, it seems as if *flexplace*—working from home—would be an ideal situation. The technology we are accustomed to using—computers, fax, phones—makes the concept workable. The "gee whiz" gadgetry that can be tacked on to standard equipment makes it seem like you can do most anything from anywhere.

In many cases, that's true. For people whose work requires concentration, quiet, and little face-to-face interaction with colleagues or customers, an office can be a lousy place to get anything accomplished.

But productivity is not the only reason behind the surge in telecommuting's popularity and its acceptance as a viable alternative work arrangement. Companies have immediate and pressing reasons to implement such a program.

Cost

If telecommuting is widespread in an organization, less office space (with its corresponding drop in overhead) is needed. Thus, operating costs can be reduced substantially, especially in high-cost urban areas.

A telecommuting program also preserves natural resources and saves the company fines it might have to pay if it didn't comply with state and federal Clean Air regulations aimed at reducing air pollution and traffic congestion.

Increasing Employee Base

Telecommuting supports diversity initiatives by broadening the employee base to include people with disabilities and parents who want to be nearer to their children during the day. These are two important pools of employees that companies want to tap into.

Turnover rates are down when employees have the option of telecommuting. When people can't stand their commutes another moment, have new family responsibilities, or have a disability that would make daily travel a hardship, they'd often rather telecommute a day or more a week than look for a new job closer to home. From the company's point of view, lower turnover means reduced recruiting and training costs.

Absenteeism

Absenteeism drops among telecommuters. Telecommuters average one less sick day a year than their office-bound counterparts. Not surprising. Semi-ill employees may not come in to the office or come in and infect a whole department. Telecommuters might snooze a few hours and then go to their home desks to work. On snowy days, employees may opt out of work rather than spend an hour shoveling their driveway to get the car out of the garage; telecommuters merely don a sweat suit and sit down at their home computers. When kids are sick, employees often use their sick days to stay home with them; telecommuters can take time out of the caregiving role when children are sleeping or quietly playing to do some work.

Relocation

The telecommuting option enables a company to keep valuable employees when it relocates its offices. A move, even if it's only 15 miles away, can put additional commuting pressure on people already stretched to the max. Rather than losing good people to companies located nearer their homes, companies with a telecommuting option can keep them. This affords a company continuity during a time of upheaval.

Telecommuters' Buzz Talk

The jargon of the virtual office (any place other than the traditional office space) needs some getting used to. Here's a selection of the new phrases.

Drop-in office: An office used in turn by many different employees. Sometimes referred to as a *satellite office* or a *telecommuting center,* this office is usually outside of high-rent big cities and closer to where employees live. It is usually set up with computers, modems and faxes.

Empowerment: A political notion applied to office organization. At the practical level, it refers to having the equipment to link up with other workers.

Face Time: Time spent face-to-face with clients, colleagues or customers.

Groupware: A category of computer software designed to allow many people to work simultaneously on a single document, plan, or spreadsheet. The best-known groupware program is Lotus Notes.

Harbors and Commons: A system of organizing private spaces and shared meeting rooms.

Hotelling: Setting up offices for temporary use, like hotel rooms. Employees make "reservations" for an office through a "concierge." Often used by consulting firms whose employees spend a great deal of time working at a client's office.

Mission Critical: Essential to getting the job done. The latest buzzword replaces "user friendly" and "state of the art."

Nonterritorial: Shared, to describe office equipment or space.

Off Site: Out of the office.

Virtual Water Cooler: Some device, perhaps a videophone, to keep those working at home linked to the camaraderie and office grapevine.

War Room: A comfortable room where people gather to strategize (not to have a traditional meeting around a conference table).

Part-time Workforce

Telecommuting works splendidly for a company needing a part-time workforce serving phone customers at odd or interrupted hours during the day. Suppose, for example, a catalog company needs extra phone operators between 7:00 and 10:00 a.m. and 6:00 and 9:00 p.m. Rather than having people congregate at the worksite at these times (and having to commute for three hours of work), these part-timers can be linked into the system and handle phone orders conveniently from their homes.

Emergency Situations

A well-established telecommuting program proves invaluable during catastrophic times, such as earthquakes, floods, fires, or even bomb scares. Unable to reach the office because of damaged roads or buildings, people who are set up to work from home are able to carry on the business of doing business. Companies with employees who telecommute improve their ability to recover from emergencies.

What's in It for Employees?

Outside, the sun was toasting the pavements and forcing the buds to open on Japanese maples. Inside, in a darkly paneled austere room, a group of managers were asked if they would like to work from home. A quick glimpse out the windows and 95 percent of them rang out with a hearty "yes." The bantering that followed ranged from, "Just give me the opportunity," to, "I'd work like the dickens with a beer in one hand and a book in the other."

But when the group started to talk specifically about what working from home would actually mean, their enthusiasm was tempered.

> "Right now I can always pop in to someone else's office to talk through an idea, and those talks net something more than I could come up with myself."

"I would be sorely tempted to forego the work and hang out at the gym or in the backyard."

"I'd feel out of the mainstream of the corporate life."

"I don't have the space to set up an office at home."

"Home is more stressful than the office."

"My family and friends wouldn't think I was 'working' if I were home. They wouldn't leave me alone."

"I know me. I have to have a clear line between work and home, or I'll wind up working in my home office all times of the day and night."

Lures and Pitfalls

What we learn from this group is that while working from home is tempting, it's not for everyone. When Apple Computer first introduced its telecommuting pilot program, for example, it expected to be inundated with requests from employees. But it got fewer than half as many takers as anticipated. The reason: Quite a number of people simply did not want to work at home or felt that they needed the social environment of the office.

The lures of telecommuting are strong; so are the pitfalls.

Lure: People are better able to balance work and family life. Shortened commuting time allows them more time with family and friends.

Pitfall: They may be tempted to give up child-care arrangements, which would severely interfere with their productivity.

Lure: Telecommuters save money and time commuting.

Pitfall: Employees may work longer hours and wind up being burned out. Instead of "getting a life," they sometimes end up with no life outside of work.

Lure: They can develop a schedule that is best for their own personal work rhythms.

Pitfall: They may not be as available or as alert when coworkers, supervisors, and customers need them.

Lure: Leading the "open collar" life increases job satisfaction.

Pitfall: Because they're not in a company setting all the time, they can lose sight of the corporate mission and its spirit.

Lure: They are not as bothered by unnecessary meetings.

Pitfall: They may not meet frequently enough with coworkers to satisfy their emotional or information needs.

Lure: They can work in pajamas or jeans—can sneeze, wheeze, or cough with abandon.

Pitfall: They may be less businesslike in their thinking if they feel too relaxed.

Lure: They're removed from the group and can concentrate better.

Pitfall: Their presence may be a catalyst for creative group thinking.

Research Your Company's Policies

Even before someone comes to you seeking permission to telecommute (whether it's working from home once a week or five times a week) or before you introduce the option to employees who you supervise, you need to be familiar with your company's policies on, and selection criteria for, telecommuting.

Eligibility

What are your company's eligibility criteria for alternative work arrangements?

Is this limited to certain levels of employees? Sometimes unions don't allow telecommuting, so it's limited only to management-level employees.

Is there a requirement that an employee must be with the company for a specific period of time? Often, a company will require a tenure of a year or more.

Are there conditions for participation? Some companies require space at home for a formal office; others insist that telecommuters have a computer and a separate business line.

Are there performance requirements that must be met?

Some companies offer telecommuting only to employees whose performance rating is satisfactory or above. This requirement often acts as an incentive for improvement for an employee with a mediocre performance record.

Issues

Know what the company's position is on as many of the telecommuting issues as possible.

► Benefits and Compensation

How are these affected by telecommuting? They shouldn't be, unless there's a decrease in responsibilities and hours.

► Liability and Insurance

Who is responsible for workers injured while working at home? Will worker's compensation cover telecommuters at home? Will telecommuters have to increase their homeowners coverage? Some companies cover workers in their home offices, but not in the rest of the house. Others include kitchens. What about coverage for equipment? Who covers stolen or damaged equipment?

► Equipment and Supplies

Is the company or the employee responsible for providing and purchasing equipment? All companies work this differently; very often departments within the same company have different policies! It often depends upon how extensive the telecommuting arrangement is; what type of work is being done at home; how much proprietary equipment, supplies and software are needed. Some companies provide each telecommuter with a customized personal computer work station and all the necessary software; others expect the telecommuter to foot the expenses of any needed equipment. The costs for setting up a telecommuter in a home-based office can range from almost nothing if the worker already has his or her own equipment (and 75 percent of U.S. telecommuters do), to a few hundred dollars to provide the necessary and linking software, to many thousands if a company provides a full-fledged setup from scratch—furniture and all.

At-Home Furniture

Here is a list of manufacturers offering home office furniture solutions and products. Suggest to your organization that it work with these companies and others to secure the best prices on office furniture for the telecommuters.

Haworth in Holland, Michigan (616) 393-3000. Home office furniture solution called "Crossings."

Summerland in Summerland Key, Florida (305) 745-1696. Manufacture's "The Office" for telecommuters.

Sligh Furniture in Holland, Michigan (616) 394-9390. Manufacture's "File-A-Way Desk" for home office.

Herman Miller, New York showroom (212) 951-3600. Home office furniture also sold in Crate & Barrel.

Steelcase in Grand Rapids, Michigan (616) 247-2710. Manufacture's "Personal Harbor" for home office use.

Vogel Peterson in Garden Grove, California (714) 895-7373. Computer cart for telecommuters called "Docking Station."

Nucraft in Comstock Park, Michigan (616) 784-6016. Makes multimedia furniture and computer carts.

Anthro in Tualatin, Oregon (800) 325-3841. Manufactures computer support furniture for the home.

—Adapted from *Interiors Magazine*

► **Overtime**

Will overtime be allowed for telecommuters? If so, how will it work? (Some companies won't pay overtime; others insist that telecommuters get permission ahead of time to put in overtime.)

► **Expenses**

What expenses will be covered? Phone? Additional electricity? Travel to the office to pick up supplies?

Safety Checklist for Telecommuters

This list should be updated periodically and kept on file with the company.

Date _____

	Yes	If no, comment
Fire Protection:		
Smoke Alarm	_____	_____
Clear access to fire extinguisher	_____	_____
Emergency Procedures:		
Evacuation plan in place	_____	_____
First aid supplies handy and adequate	_____	_____
Electrical:		
Extension cords in good condition	_____	_____
Cords and cables secured and not a tripping hazard	_____	_____
Outlets grounded and not overloaded	_____	_____
Surge protection	_____	_____
Surricient ventilation for electrical equipment	_____	_____
Fuse box accessible and properly labeled	_____	_____
Workspace:		
Work area uncluttered	_____	_____
Equipment protected from direct light and heat	_____	_____
Workspace has adequate light and temperature control	_____	_____
Furniture sturdy and adjusted properly	_____	_____

► Safety Requirements

Does the company have safety requirements for the home office? Will ergonomic requirements be set, such as for lighting, desk heights or chairs? Some companies provide consultants to help employees set up a home office; others have inspections. At the very least, provide an employee with a home safety checklist, such as the one provided in this section.

► Back-up Arrangements

What will employees do if their home equipment malfunctions? Even though most people are adept at using the equipment, many are all thumbs when fixing it. Some companies have a hotline into their Information Systems Department; others expect employees to set up their own safety net. Some are given training in how to use the equipment and basic information on how to correct the most common glitches.

Special Concerns

There are a few areas of special interest that may introduce barriers to a telecommuting arrangement. They should be investigated and resolved before continuing such an arrangement.

Upfront Costs

Telecommuting is one of the few alternative work arrangements that could have an up-front outlay. The company should have done a cost/benefit analysis before instituting a policy, but you might have to do one for your own department. Include in that analysis the potential costs and the potential savings.

Among the potential costs are program development (your time and anyone else's involved in developing a telecommuting program); equipment/service/furniture costs; and management and employee training costs.

Among the potential savings to consider are office space or furniture saving; utility and security savings; recruitment savings (if you can keep good employees you may have lost otherwise), training savings (if you increase retention, you save on costs of training new hires); compliance with federal and state regulations; and increased productivity.

Union Objections

Some union leaders object to telecommuting. They are concerned about the impact on union solidarity. And the history of work-at-home has been tainted by past abuses. But most union members today don't have that historical perspective. They see telecommuting as a viable work arrangement in today's environment. So they are pushing labor leaders to come around to the idea. Bringing the union into the planning and policy process early on helps overcome the leadership's resistance.

Sensitive Material

Companies often worry about sensitive material that an employee might take home or would be able to access from a home computer. First, security is an issue that should be addressed with Information Systems and/or a security consultant early in any telecommuting initiative. Second, employees must be cautioned that confidential material worked on at home must also be protected from people who have access to their computers. When they are not at their desks, sensitive documents must be out of view and safely stored. Sensitive computer files should be protected by setting up a password to gain access or having a lock installed on the hard drive.

Getting Started

After you have done your research on your company's policy and are pretty well convinced your organization could handle an alternative work arrangement, you will need to match this to a candidate. What are the barriers managers see?

How and when can I say "no" to a telecommuting request? It would be inappropriate to say "no" simply because you don't think the employee has the temperament to work at home. But you certainly can say "no" if the employee doesn't meet the company's participation requirements. In fact, you have the responsibility to say "no" if there's a valid business reason to say "no." Among those reasons:

- The employee needs to be available to customers who come into the office.

- The employee works as part of a team and his or her physical presence is a vital part of the success of that team.

- The information the employee works with may be too sensitive to leave the office or access on a home computer.

In addition, some jobs just can't be done while working at home. You can't be a company nurse while sitting at your home computer, for example.

If I can't see someone, how do I know he or she is really working? Most managers don't actually "see" work being done, especially when most of the work is done at the computer or at a desk. We measure most people's worth to the organization and department not by how much we see them but by what they accomplish.

Will an employee work less while unsupervised? Studies indicate that employees who are well suited to telecommuting tend to work *more* when unsupervised, not *less.* In fact, one of the reasons telecommuters bow out of this arrangement is that they don't take regular breaks, they work long into the evening, and they wind up burning out because of overwork.

How will this arrangement affect employees who are not telecommuting? How in-office colleagues view the arrangement depends in large measure upon how the supervisor views it. Coworkers are more likely to view the arrangement as "normal" if they can do the following:

- Keep the telecommuter in the loop

- View him or her as a vital member of the department

- Maintain close communication ties with the telecommuter

- Are apprised of the telecommuter's schedule

- Feel the telecommuter is flexible in amending that schedule if necessary

- They are asked for feedback in how to make the process work even better

To ensure colleagues' cooperation they must not be laden with the telecommuter's in-office responsibilities—unless they've agreed to exchange some elements of their jobs with the telecommuter.

Preparing the Proposal

Ask the employee to think through the following, covering all points in specific terms, and put it in the form of a written proposal. (You will need to allow some meeting time with the candidate to clarify your expectations and apprise him or her of any company policies of which they might not be aware.)

Which job tasks can be done at home and which are best done at the office? _____

_____

_____

How many days a week and which ones will he or she be working from home? Will there be core hours during which he or she will be available? _____

_____

_____

How he or she will stay in touch with coworkers, you and clients/customers? _____

_____

_____

What are performance expectations for the job? _____

_____

_____

What criteria will be used in evaluating productivity and performance? _____

_____

_____

How often will you review performance during the pilot period?

_____

_____

_____

How long should a pilot program last? How will you and the employee work together to improve the arrangement as it needs fine-turning? _____

_____

_____

Remember, you and the telecommuter need to have a work agreement that specifies certain critical details, including work goals, the length of the telecommuting arrangement, the daily schedule, methods of communication, expectations about the employee's presence in the office, and conditions of promotion.

Modern Technology's Gee-Whiz Gadgetry

Although some people can work at home with just a pad, pencil and phone, here is a sampling of what's available for those in need of somewhat higher-tech mechanisms (which get more sophisticated daily). Rest assured that technology development is moving so quickly that many alternatives exist for extending the corporate networks into the home. The approach your company and you, the manager, will take depends on the user's needs.

BASIC COMPONENTS: Phone, computer, fax

ADD-ON APPARATUS:

Voice mail gives you enormous flexibility with the phone: from afar you can access messages, reply to them, forward them, respond to a particular person, etc.

Cellular phones allow you to stay in phone contact no matter where you are—in the car, boat, bathroom. Laptop computers with built-in fax-modem boards give you the flexibility to take your office with you everywhere you go.

Pagers can contact you when you're out of phone reach. You can get one for use on the ground, another for use on airplane flights.

Modems connect to PCs and phone lines and enable you to send and receive data to others who also have modems.

On-line services get you into the electronic mail routine, allow you access to up-to-the-minute research, and encourage swapping of ideas with people all over the world.

PHONE WONDERS:

Here are some of the services telephone companies offer.

Call forwarding allows calls to follow you around and helps keep the division between office and home (or anywhere else) transparent.

Call answering is like an answering machine because it takes calls when your line is busy.

Caller ID acts as a secretary and lets you know who's calling before you pick up the phone.

Voice dialing allows you to place a call by merely saying the name.

High-speed interconnectivity for PCs can be as simple or as complex as you need.

Desktop videoconferencing allows you to communicate verbally and visually. You can see the person you're communicating with and/or documents that you're talking about.

Personal phone numbers that use a new "500" area code go with you wherever you are.

Increased Sales: A Success Story

At an international "teleworking" conference held in late 1994 in San Francisco, Eric Hodson, a British telework consultant reported that it cost American Express Travel Services in Houston about $1,300 to set up one home office. But Amex travel sales agents working at home handled 26 percent more calls and generated 46 percent more sales, so the initial cost plus the telecommunications charges that Amex picked up were more than offset by the increase in sales. In fact, Hodson said, each telecommuting Amex agent generates about $30,000 more a year in sales than his or her central office counterpart.

?

No Easy Answers—No Right Answers

How would you handle these situations? Keep in mind some of the many factors to consider: the needs of your department, your corporate culture, how valuable the employee is to your organization, the morale of you department.

What Do You Think?

You try to reach a telecommuter by phone for hours and the line is busy. When you finally get through, the telecommuter's teenage daughter answers and tells you her dad is out on an appointment. It's obvious that she's been on her father's line all this time.

Should you tell her to stay off the business line, tell her father about the situation when you speak to him later, or stay out of it?

What Do You Think?

Two telecommuters with overlapping schedules share an office and all the office equipment. They ask you if the department will purchase a laptop, so that one of them can work on it in the conference room when both are in the office at the same time.

Do you consider that a reasonable request?

What Do You Think?

A person in your department requests a telecommuting schedule for four days a week. This person spends a great deal of time socializing in the office and you don't think he is a self-starter.

Would you refuse the request?

What Do You Think?

A certain employee is a great informal leader among her peers. She asks for a schedule that will have her working from home three days a week.

Do you think it's reasonable to refuse because you think her absence might have a detrimental effect on your department's functioning?

Chapter 7

Job Sharing: A Team Approach

Job sharing is so frequently written about that you would think everyone is doing it. Not so. The complexity and the reduced pay and benefits of the arrangement make it unsuitable for most people. While this alternative arrangement is on the upswing, especially among clerical, administrative, professional and managerial women who want to devote more time to rearing children (but plan to come back to fulltime work in the future), it's not a frequently evoked arrangement. That's probably because this, of all the alternative work arrangements, is the most complicated to arrange and raises the most skepticism among managers. Yet when it works well, job sharing has enormous benefits to the company and provides the employees with a balance beam to the work-life dilemma.

Different from two part-time employees who have specific responsibilities independent of one other, job sharers act as a team and share the responsibilities of one fulltime position. Also different is the perception: two people working part-time implies a splintered effort and impact; two job sharers working together share a common vision and bring to the position extensive coverage and creative problem-solving abilities.

When job sharing works out, the company is able to retain valuable employees and maintain staffing continuity. There is increased productivity and reduced burnout. Job sharers use each other to problem-solve, coming up with more viable solutions than either could separately. Employee motivation, loyalty and commitment swells. "I thought I had died and gone to heaven when the company agreed to the arrangement." said one. "I couldn't work at a better place."

Who Is a Likely Candidate?

Who would want this arrangement? Consider these pairs, for whom the arrangement has worked well.

▶ When NBC was looking for one fulltime, on-air news correspondent, two visible TV personalities teamed up for the job. One was a correspondent for another news show on the same network; the other had been a reporter and anchorwoman on another network. Their reason: both were new mothers looking for a way to mesh family life with the heavy demands of on-camera reporting.

▶ Two administrative assistants in the legal department of a large insurance company now share one administrative assistant job. Why? One wanted to go back to school part-time and spend more time with her two school-aged sons; the other wanted to start a home-based business and spend time with his newborn son.

▶ When the associate director of development at a large NYC hospital went on maternity leave, the position was temporarily filled by a freelance writer/book author. Three months after the baby was born, the associate director wanted to come back to work—but not on a full-time basis. Her replacement during the three months had enjoyed filling in, but didn't want to commit to fulltime work because of her writing. The positive solution for both women and for the hospital: job sharing.

Challenges to Job Sharers

In a report issued by The Conference Board in New York, job sharers indicated their greatest challenges centered around

- differing work styles and quality standards

- the effect of the arrangement on their career advancement

- difficulty staying in touch with one another

- inequality of the work load

- dominance of one partner

The perfect fit between colleagues is as difficult as the perfect marriage. It requires melding work styles. Sometimes different styles complement each other, such as when one person is slow, methodical, and pays attention to details and the other is good at broad stoking and meeting deadlines. However, the arrangement works best when job sharers have similar styles: two dogged individuals; two detail people; two self-starters. If they can't dovetail their different styles or come to terms on a style that works for both of them, they'll wind up unproductive, frustrated, and resentful. The arrangement won't work if one job sharer promptly returns customer calls and the other procrastinates. Or if one keeps meticulous, written customer records and the other stores information in her head.

Both must be excellent communicators. Naturally, each has to share a detailed record of what happened on her "watch." It can be done through e-mail, note pad, phone, or face-to-face meetings. Charts of pending projects can be made and updated daily to show at a glance what each person has been doing and how far toward completion the project is.

But it's not just the nuts and bolts of what happened that must be communicated. The nuances—such as how a customer sounded on the phone, why one thought their supervisor kept poking her head into the office, what a client said about his daughter's wedding—also have to be shared.

Job sharers have to be flexible. Because they are operating as a team, if one knows in advance that she will have to be out on a day she's expected to be in, the other is expected to cover. If they're both needed to close a deal or if one works better with a customer who will be in town on a day she's supposed to be off, schedules are usually shuffled to accommodate business needs. Numerous time configurations can be worked out, but the most frequently cited ones are (1) one person works mornings, the other afternoons; (2) one person works one week, the other the next week; or (3) one works Monday through Wednesday, till 1:00 p.m.; the other Wednesday noon through Friday—overlapping for a debriefing lunch.

They have to have similar career aspirations and hopes for advancement. Job sharers need to discuss this before the arrangement is put in place. They may agree that they're not interested in promotions during their job-sharing stint because they don't want additional responsibility at this time. Or they may see themselves as a team on the way up and market themselves as a high-performing matched pair ready to take on whatever new challenges they can.

They have to respect and trust one another. Each has to feel the other is pulling her own weight. And when things go especially well, they have to be comfortable sharing the glory and the spotlight. When things go wrong, they must share the responsibility and not be ready to point the finger at the other.

Challenges to Managers

Continued management skepticism and resistance to job sharing is stunting the arrangement's growth, however. Managers object to the

- Increased burden of supervising two employees

- Increased costs associated with job sharing

- Increased headcount

- Possible difficulty of meeting client and customer needs

A manager's willingness to problem-solve and adapt his or her supervising style to accommodate the arrangement goes a long way in making job sharing work.

Managers fear more work because now they will be supervising two employees instead of one. On some level that is true. You will have an additional performance review and you'll have to think about evaluating people on their individual performance as well as their ability to work as a member of a job sharing team.

But over the long haul, there's probably less supervision required. Job sharers understand (and the manager must emphasize the fact, when needed) that they are responsible for making the arrangement work. Initially, coordination problems need to be worked out. But if the pair is well suited and understands the responsibilities of the job (and how they are going to divide up these responsibilities), they are usually more self-motivated and conscientious than other employees.

Increased Costs

Job sharing can represent added costs in terms of benefits to additional employees and their families. But managers can fairly and truthfully rationalize that increase by contending the costs are offset by lower turnover and higher productivity. The idea that a manager has to count both halves of the same position as two people is ludicrous. Companies committed to alternative work arrangements are converting their methods of budgeting for staff from "head count" to "fulltime equivalent."

Client Satisfaction

Clients and customers have to be fully informed of the arrangement and know who is going to deal with them if the person handling that aspect of the job isn't in. Unless customers are fully convinced that both parts of the team are committed to servicing them, they'll be dissatisfied with the arrangement.

It makes all parties more comfortable if job sharers have face-to-face meetings with customers to reassure them of their commitment to service. When a team is working on all cylinders, clients are usually thrilled with the fact that they have access to two skilled people who know them—and not just one. It's a value-added arrangement.

Employees' Responsibilities

When one employee broaches the job-share concept, the supervisor should ask her to identify all the key responsibilities of the position and also to sketch, in words, an outline of what she would consider an ideal partner. Bringing in the human resources department at that time will hasten the search for a partner since the department has a better picture of employees within the company and probably knows of another would-be job sharer. In their efforts to identify a partner, some companies combine a formal job posting system with informal networking. Some will even advertise or seek the job sharer from outside the company, but that's rare.

Most of the time the job sharing request is initiated by two employees who have already discussed the concept between themselves and have thought it out fairly well. The two might not hold the same position in the company; they might not even be from the same department. They may simply be two people interested in reducing their work hours while still feeling that they are doing meaningful work. They may have already decided on which of their two jobs they would like to share. One may be eager to veer in a different career direction or learn skills she wouldn't have learned in the position she now holds. They may be at different levels within the organization and be at different salary levels.

In any case, when a potential job sharing pair makes a formal presentation to you, the manager, they should include the following—with explanations and specifics:

1. The benefits to the company and the department

2. A proposed schedule

3. A proposed division of duties, including cross-coverage

4. A communications plan

5. Proposed salaries and benefits

6. Proposed dissolution plan

Job Sharing Checklist

Even if you as a manager are convinced of the worth of a job-sharing arrangement, you will want to explore in depth the following with the potential job sharers before an arrangement is put into place.

Tasks and Responsibilities

Specifically, how will the responsibilities and workload be divided? Will there be much time lost due to duplication of work and the need for close communication? Consider the following:

- Are the job sharers' communications strategies well thought out and sufficient to assure a smooth flow of information between them, coworkers, and clients or customers?

- How and when will they establish priorities?

- Do they both know the responsibilities of the job well? Will one or both of them need additional training?

- How will vacations, holidays, and sick time be handled? Will they be flexible enough to cover for each other during vacations and sick days? Will their flexibility extend to peak periods or emergency situations?

- How will work space be shared, especially if there's an overlap of time when both are in the office?

- How will client satisfaction with the arrangement be evaluated?

Compensation Issues

Surprising as it seems at first, job sharers might not be compensated equally. Compensation will depend upon:

- Their experience, capabilities, and expertise.

- Whether one's volume of work is considerably greater than the other's.

- How they're evaluated (jointly, jointly and individually, or individually).

- How many hours they work.

- How much the manager has in the budget to pay for the position and the benefits included in the package.

- Their seniority within an organization.

Sometimes job sharers receive a prorated share of the salary and full benefits; others receive a prorated share both of the salary and the benefits. (To receive full benefits many companies require job sharers to work a minimum of 20 hours.)

Job sharers should be eligible for bonuses and promotions based on performance reviews in the same manner regular employees are.

Dissolution Issues

What happens when one job sharer (or you the manager) wants to dissolve the job-sharing arrangement for any one of the following reasons?

- One or both of the job sharers may move to a new job.

- One of the job sharers is terminated or resigns.

- Business conditions dictate that the shared job be returned to one fulltime position or eliminated entirely.

- One or both job sharers, or management, decides that the job-sharing arrangement is not working.

The issue of dissolution should be dealt with beforehand—with written guidelines—since the majority of job share arrangements will not last indefinitely. In fact, most average two years in length; few last up to five years.

When one person leaves (or is asked to leave), most companies handle the transition in one of these ways:

- The remaining person may continue for whatever would be a reasonable time to recruit a replacement. Some companies require that the remaining person revert to fulltime during the recruiting process.

- The job sharer, the supervisor, and human resources look for a person, either in the same department or a different one, who might be a suitable replacement.

- If a suitable partner cannot be found, the remaining job sharer must either revert to fulltime, leave the position, or work with human resources for placement in another part-time position.

Manager's Checklist

Asking yourself the following questions will help you determine the viability of the arrangement from your own vantage point and that of the company's.

- What are the job-sharing arrangement's real benefits to the company?

- Does the plan the job sharers have presented identify potential problems and solutions? Does it address individual strengths and weaknesses? Compatibility? Team effectiveness?

- Is the plan specific enough to give you a good basis for evaluating each job sharer's performance? Will you be able to rate each job sharer separately on individual performance and on the ability to work as a member of a team.

- If additional training is needed, what will it cost and who will do it?

- Will additional compensation be necessary for extra days or hours? If so, how does that fit into the budget?

Common Problems: Possible Solutions

Problem: *The job sharers are in a managerial position and the people reporting to them test them to see if one will give the same response as the other.*

Solutions: Job sharers must be in sync on their commitment to common goals and objectives by discussing them regularly. They must devise a way to get in touch with each other at any time to discuss a particular situation requiring immediate action that they're not sure how to handle because it involves something the other is working on.

They should be up front with employees about the fact that they operate as a team. "I'll have to check with Janice to see how it will affect what she's working on before I can give you an answer."

Problem: *One job sharer appears to be pulling more weight than the other.*

Solutions: Discuss with them their responsibility to make the job-sharing arrangement work more equitably.

Adjust assignments to balance the workload or adjust salary to reflect the different contributions.

As a last resort, single out for reward or recognize one of the job sharers for her particular performance.

Problem: *Job sharers have become so compatible that they're swapping time frequently. You, their colleagues, and their customers don't know who is in the office when.*

Solutions: Have them prepare a calendar listing their schedules and ask them to distribute it to you and anyone else in or outside the organization who has contact with them.

Permit them to swap time only with your prior knowledge and approval.

Job Sharing Systems

According to a survey of 131 corporations, academic and government agencies, and consultants, done by The Conference Board in New York, six types of systems are of particular help in supervising job-sharing arrangements:

- *Formal written guidelines or checklists*

- *A job-sharing agreement or contract*

- *A system for holding job sharers accountable*

- *A system for arranging coverage*

- *A system for clear and consistent communication*

- *Management training*

Having these in place will give you the support you need to make the arrangement a successful one.

?

No Easy Answers—No Right Answers

How would you handle this situation? Keep in mind some of the many factors to consider: the needs of your department, your corporate culture, how valuable the employee is to your organization, the morale of your department.

What Do You Think?

A client complains to you about a job-sharing arrangement because he wants fulltime service by one representative.

How would you respond? Would you eliminate the job-sharing arrangement even if you think it's working well?

Chapter 8

Reducing the Workweek When an Employee "Can't Do It All"

More and more people see a voluntary reduction in the number of hours worked as a way of more effectively balancing work and personal lives. Even those who have yet to start families or who have no immediate plans for families of their own are sounding a bit like Oliver Twist. "More," they are saying. "May I have more, please." Only instead of food, these people are asking for time. Generation X, those in their 20s who have just entered the job market are particularly cynical of the long hours their parents spent in the workplace while they were growing up. From their perspective, the baby boomers sold out their principles and placed work ahead of family—and money-making over personal development and commitment to community.

Some U.S. companies are railing against the idea of people working a reduced workweek—for a number of reasons. Many pay all or a large part of their workers' health benefits. Hiring more workers (two to do the job of one, for example) would mean higher health-care costs, even if the share was prorated, they assume. (Actually, according to a Bureau of National Affairs Special Report, analyses of part-time and job-sharing arrangements showed no significant additional cost, particularly when companies had modified employee benefits plans and they had a full-time equivalency system rather than a headcount system.)

Organizations also are concerned about the implications and complications of the arrangement on customer relations. Customers accustomed to dealing with one employee might find themselves lost in a sea of "but-that's-not-my-responsibility" answers when their regular contact is not around. If that happens, it's frustrating for the consumer, and downright catastrophic for business. So, instead of using part-timers, a number of companies shrink their workforce and rely on the overtime of their already skeletal staff to perform the tasks.

Reducing Wasted Time on the Job

Then there's the more positive view of people working on a reduced schedule. Some companies view the growing number of people who want to work part-time as a boon.

From the companies' point of view, plenty of fulltime jobs can be done on a part-time basis. Senior management is vaguely aware of the amount of goof-off time some employees enjoy. In a recent *Money* magazine poll, a sizable minority of American wage earners admitted that they're somewhat less diligent than they should be. Fifteen percent said they spend between 10 and 20 percent of their time at work goofing off; 4 percent spend between 20 and 50 percent, and a brazen 3 percent indicated that they spend more than half their workday doing nothing. The challenge, of course, is ferreting out the band of do-very-littlers and linking them with enough part-time work to bring them somewhat up to speed. Chances are that's not what's going to happen, however.

Two-Income Families

Many people are opting for this partial involvement in the workforce, especially two-income families with children. Their rationale: The income associated with working fulltime doesn't justify the costs of child care, commuting, eating out frequently (too tired to cook!), and most importantly, time away from the family. Companies find that accommodating an employee's request for a reduced schedule can make the difference between retaining and losing a good employee.

Downsizing

Voluntarily reducing hours is one way to ease the pain of downsizing. In union companies, union members have often backed the idea of spreading the work to people who would otherwise be laid off.

Reduced Workweek Options

A variety of ways exist for shortening the workweek: part-time work and voluntarily reduced work time, which includes phasing in and phasing out.

Regular Part-Time

This is less than fulltime work by employees on a company's regular payroll, and is a long-term arrangement. Ideally, part-time offers the same degree of job security and a pro rata share of the rights and

Benefits of Part-Timers Compared with Those of Fulltimers		
Benefits	**% of Part-Time* Workers Eligible**	**% of Fulltime Workers Eligible**
Paid vacation time	55	96
Paid holidays	47	92
Paid sick leave	30	67
Paid jury duty	45	86
Paid maternity leave	1	2
Paid paternity leave	less than 0.5	1
Employee assistance programs	31	56
Flexible benefits plans	2	10
Employer-subsidized child care	5	8
Eldercare	4	9
Wellness programs	16	35
Medical insurance	28	83
Dental insurance	18	60
Life insurance	31	94
Retirement plans	40	78

*Employees are classified as part-time in accordance with practices of surveyed establishments.

SOURCE: U.S. Bureau of Labor Statistics, Employee Benefits in Medium and Large Private Establishments, 1991.

benefits available to the fulltime workers. But not always. When discussing the most-sought-after benefit—health care—a few companies contend that everyone working for them, part-time or fulltime, is eligible. In fact, according to the Bureau of National Affairs Special Report, companies offering full benefits for part-time work felt that the benefits outweighed the costs. Among those benefits: a predictable source of part-time workers with expertise and savings of administrative costs associated with implementing prorated benefits. Other companies limit eligibility to those working 20 or 25 hours a week; others limit eligibility to only fulltimers.

Voluntarily Reduced Time

This is thought of as a temporary arrangement, whereby the employee has every intention of coming back fulltime in a few months—usually defined by companies as three months. The reduction is usually sparked by an immediate or emergency need for time. A family situation that requires more of the employee's time, such as providing care for, or being with a terminally ill parent, may be the reason for a reduced work schedule request. In those cases, where the limit of the reduced schedule is clearly defined, benefits usually remain intact, though compensation would be affected.

Phasing In and Phasing Out

Two outgrowths of voluntary reduced time are phasing in and phasing out.

Phasing in, or coming back to work on a reduced work schedule after you've been out, has been a long-accepted workplace practice, especially when it's used for people coming back to work after an illness. Someone returning to work after being out for bypass surgery, for example, might come back to work only partial days for a couple of months. Now phasing in is also being used by new parents, who, after taking maternity or paternity leave, may want to ease themselves back to work on a reduced schedule for the next three months. It may be used in conjunction with other leaves. For example, a utilities company has the following graduated phasing-in policy available for women on maternity leave. It involves four phases: family and medical leave; part-time with work at home; fulltime with some work at home; and finally full time in the office. Interestingly, the Bureau of National Affairs' Special

Report indicates a cost saving for companies allowing a phase-in for new mothers that hadn't been anticipated: more than half the women interviewed said part-time jobs enabled them to take shorter leaves.

Phasing out is a form of reduced workweek, usually associated with people nearing retirement age. It helps companies take advantage of the experience of seasoned employees at the same time the employees get themselves psychologically ready for a drastic lifestyle change.

Getting the Benefits Facts

Because reducing the workweek has an effect on compensation and/or benefits, managers must make certain all employees requesting this arrangement think it through carefully and check with the Human Resources department to get all the details relating to benefit changes.

Concerns About Part-Time

As a manager, you might be concerned that a part-timer would be less productive and less committed to the company and less committed to doing a good job. Put your concerns to rest. Studies indicate that people who request the reduction appreciate the company's flexibility and are more committed and productive than they had been before. For the growing number of professionals joining the ranks of part-timers, the arrangement is a way for them to continue to develop their skills and abilities on the job while still balancing work and personal lives. People with young families especially view part-time in a more favorable light. No longer do they feel work is an "all or nothing" proposition. (Keep in mind, though, that while part-time may be the answer when someone is suffering from burnout or conflicting work-family obligations, it's not the answer if an employee's performance is weak. Working fewer hours won't improve poor motivation, lack of interest, inadequate training or lack of ability.)

Paring a job down from full- to part-time is not always easy and not always possible. Many questions emerge about its feasibility.

▶ *What's the nature of the job? Is it project-oriented? Does a certain portion of it have to be done every day?*

If the job requires a lot of communication with other divisions, frequent travel, or consistent customer/client contact, it might not be possible to do it on a part-time basis . . . unless there's a possibility that the person requesting part-time would be able to job share.

▶ *Can managers and supervisors have a part-time position?*

It's possible and it happens. When a supervisor has a limited number of employees to manage, is comfortable delegating work, has solid communication skills, and has back-up management on the premises to handle problems when he or she is not there, it can work well. Because many managers work longer than the traditional 40-hour week, it's important to think of a reduced work schedule in terms of percent of tasks, not percent of hours. This way, the manager has definite responsibilities that must be accounted for. Additional responsibilties can be assumed if time allows or other provisions for accomplishing them must be made.

▶ *What about professionals?*

People who work on a case-by-case or project-by-project basis can scale back their work fairly easily. Attorneys can handle fewer cases; accountants fewer accounts; consultants fewer clients.

▶ *How will head counts be handled?*

Companies who understand that alternative work arrangements are the wave of the future for human resources management and that the policy will be a powerful force in attracting, motivating, and retaining valuable employees, have altered the headcount policy for flexible work arrangement policies and count a part-time employee as one-half of a position so that headcount won't be affected. If that's not how it is at your company, speak to human resources to see if the policy can be changed. Otherwise, you'll worry about your ability to hire someone else to pick up the slack, and you have little incentive to grant a part-time request because you'll be over your staff limit.

When You Can't Accommodate the Request

Suppose someone asks for part-time but you're not sure you can oblige and still get all the department's work done. The department's work load is a major factor to consider in making a decision to grant the request. Upon reflection you might decide that you can accommodate a part-time position for four months, but that you can't extend it beyond that. If you and the employee concur, put the agreement in writing. If the person is unwilling or unable to return to work when needed, then the person's employ in your department would be terminated—although the human resources department might be able to find the person a reduced workweek job in another area of the company.

Can Colleagues Pick Up the Slack?

Under a voluntary reduced-time arrangement where you expect the employee to return to the fulltime job at the end of an agreed-upon time frame, you, as the supervisor, have to make a decision that requires considerable reflection: will you hire a temporary or part-time employee to handle the things that don't get done or will colleagues be able to pick up the slack?

If the additional work is too time-consuming or difficult to be done during regular hours, you may have to authorize overtime or bring in an outsider on a temporary or part-time basis to ease the overwork situation. You might also consider shifting some of the responsibilities to a more junior staff person and use the experience as part of a training program for future advancement.

If you expect colleagues to cover for the employee, what will you do to prevent resentment from fomenting? If the employee is well regarded and coworkers understand the situation, most will pick up the slack without feeling resentful—much like they would do in cases of injury or illness. But the tone is established by you, the supervisor. First, cooperation and a cross-trained workforce is something every department should strive for, not necessarily to handle just such emergencies but because these attributes are essential for departmental productivity. Second, employees have to understand that this reduced workweek is available to everyone. While they might not have to—or want to—use it now, future life problems or events might make the use of this alternative work arrangement necessary. Their cooperation now will insure others' cooperation later.

Prioritizing the Employee's Tasks

When time is scarce, the most important tasks must get done first. So you and the employee requesting a voluntary reduced schedule should both know what must be done on a daily or weekly basis versus what can be accomplished over a longer time frame. It's also important to take advantage of the particular talents this person brings to the job. If the person is especially good at a task and can do it quickly, that person should continue to assume that task. Help the person prioritize his or her responsibilities to verify that all tasks will be adequately performed during their absence.

Problem: Solution

Problem: *You know that some of the people in the department are capable of doing the work that the employee requesting a voluntarily reduced schedule is doing, but you don't have money in the budget for cross-training.*

Solution: Ask the person who's going on a reduced work schedule to train at least two others in the department to handle the tasks he or she won't be able to accomplish in the limited work arrangement.

Problem: *A supervisor in your department requested and was granted a reduced workweek. He's working four days a week instead of five. Now he comes to you complaining that while he likes the arrangement generally, he's working the same number of hours he did before (works later each evening) and gets the same amount done. As much as he appreciates the one-day-off arrangement, he doesn't think it's fair that his compensation has been reduced by 1/5th.*

Solutions: Ask him to keep a log of his activities. Is he doing more than just the essential elements? If so, help him set a limit on the number of activities assumed or the time he will spend on each. Don't push him beyond that and let his colleagues know that he's not available after certain hours.

Or, ask him if he wants to negotiate the arrangement to a compressed workweek, so that he would be compensated as a fulltime employee, working four days instead of five.

As a last resort, consider paying him an hourly rate instead of a salaried rate. That would provide you with an incentive to keep his hours to where they were supposed to be, but it might also provide him with an incentive to stretch time on the task.

New to the Rank and File: Part-Time Retirement

Phasing out people on the verge of retiring has been a blessing both to the future retirees and to the company. Most people in their 60s, 70s, and 80s who want to continue working are still vital, extraordinarily dedicated to the company, extremely skilled, and have broad experience. They just don't want to work as much or as hard as they have been. They'd like, and feel they deserve, more leisure time to enjoy their families, their homes, and their outside interests. But they still need some meaningful responsibility so they feel they're making a contribution to the company. They're not ready to fall off the employment cliff into retirement.

Some companies give these people the opportunity to transfer into less stressful jobs, often on a reduced schedule. As long as their new jobs aren't mindless and unimportant, this reduced-stress environment is a good precursor to being fully retired. The movement also makes their old positions available to up-and-coming employees in the company.

Some companies give preretirees projects to work on that tap into their broad experience and years on the firing line. Because seasoned employees have nothing to prove and no one to elbow (they don't want to move up the corporate ladder), they consider these assignments "fun."

How Companies Benefit from Preretirees

When companies have programs allowing preretirees to gradually reduce the workweek, or work on a permanently reduced workweek, either to prepare for retirement or to continue working on an abbreviated schedule after retirement age, they can capture the best of the experienced worker. Studies indicate older people are more punctual and absent less than younger workers. A particularly interesting survey of 150 people between the ages of 65 and 102 who have stayed on the job published in the book *The Longevity Factor: The New Reality of Long Careers and How It Can Lead to Richer Lives* (written by Lydia Bronte, a Manhattan gerontologist), revealed that almost half of these people had their most productive years at 50 or later and one-third said their major achievement occurred around 65.

Some companies utilize people on a reduced work schedule to act as *trainers* and *mentors* for younger people so that the skills they possess don't walk out the door when they retire.

Many companies are using retirees to fill in as needed as part of their *temporary workforce.* Insurance companies have been most innovative along these lines. They use retired personnel to process claims during peak periods, such as after the terrorist bombing in Oklahoma City, the Mississippi River floods, California fires, tornadoes in the heartlands, and hurricanes in the Southern states. The benefits of using retired people are obvious. They can step in without training because they know the ropes, have the technical expertise, and understand the corporate culture.

While many American companies have had their consciousness raised about sexism and racism and have realized how important the talents of women and minorities are to their survival, they haven't yet eliminated widely held attitudes that older workers can't do the job. But they are going to have to because older workers working in an environment of ageism won't be as productive as they might be.

Social Security and Pension Plans

Will people want to work on a reduced workweek after age 65 if their social security benefits are affected? Some will; some won't. They will have to make that determination on an individual basis.

For your information, here are the rules and regulations. For people aged 65–69, one dollar in social security benefits is withheld for every three dollars in earnings above a limit of approximately $11,500. For people under 65, one dollar in social security benefits is withheld for every two dollars in earnings above the limit of approximately $8,200. These limits change annually, so the employee will have to check out specifics with the local Social Security office or with your human resources department. After age 70, earned income doesn't affect social security.

Pensions may be affected. In most cases, pension benefits still accumulate. The rub, however, is when a company's pension plan uses the average of a person's last few years of service to calculate benefits.

Unless there's a change in the way a pension plan is written, a pre-retiree working a reduced schedule (and therefore receiving a reduced salary) will be negatively affected.

Until corporations rewrite pension plans to reflect this alternative work arrangement for preretirees and retirees, it is more likely that older people wanting to work a reduced schedule will do so as employees of a temporary or part-time agency or on a consulting basis.

Management Dilemmas and Suggestions

Dilemma: *"Call Marian. She's home with the baby, but she knows the answer to your questions."*

Suggestions: Don't expect someone to be on tap when they're out of the office because of a reduced schedule, since the very reason they're out is probably the need for freedom to handle other responsibilities. If Marian is the only one with particular knowledge of a situation (which shouldn't be the case, unless the department is tiny) or there's no one else in the organization who can be brought up to speed quickly enough to fill in, perhaps you can ask the person on a reduced schedule to call in on the days he or she is off—maybe mid-day—to answer any questions anyone has.

Dilemma: *"I hope Alison doesn't expect to waltz in here after having been out three months and spend her first week back at work catching up on the gossip she's missed."*

Suggestions: When the person begins to phase in from being out for a while, you'll need to smooth the way for a successful reentry. First, make certain you discuss your expectations regarding schedule and workload and that he or she understands them. Then, it's possible you'll want to change or shift workloads and responsibilities. Suppose, for example, the person who was filling in became very adept at some of the new tasks and handling them fit into his or her schedule very easily. You might want to reassign responsibilities—after having discussed the possibility with both parties so that everyone understands the reasons for the changes and is agreeable to them.

Dilemma: *"I'm truly impressed with the way Jackie has handled her job on a part-time basis. I'm pretty certain that she'll be back fulltime in a few years when her children start school. How can I make certain that when she does return, she gets recognition and an opportunity for advancement."*

Suggestions: You sound like a most enlightened manager, so it's likely you're already using a number of strategies, such as,

- Finding out more about her career aspirations so that even during the period that she's working on a reduced schedule, she's focused on making good career decisions.

- Making certain she gets her share of high-visibility assignments and, when she accomplishes these well, that she gets the recognition she deserves.

- Making certain she gets the promotions she deserves. She may not move as quickly as she would if she were working fulltime, but realistic advancement is possible.

- Including her in training programs or have her represent your department at company meetings or conferences.

- Suggesting that she stay in touch with colleagues at the office and help them out with extra work occasionally, and that she maintain her membership in professional organizations.

?

No Easy Answers—No Right Answers

How would you handle this situation? Keep in mind some of the many factors to consider: the needs of your department, your corporate culture, how valuable the employee is to your organization, the morale of your department.

What Do You Think?

One of your employees requests a voluntary reduced work schedule for two months because she wants to be home each day when her children come back from day camp. She tells you she'll be back to a regular schedule in September.

Would you allow her to do this every summer?

What if you discovered, on good authority, that she's really setting up a home-based business and plans to leave the company at the end of the summer? Would her future plans be a consideration in your decision to grant the request?

Chapter 9

Managing Individual Performance

A communications specialist reporting to an operations vice president at a major financial firm tells of her boss's reaction when she requested a flextime schedule so that she could come in at 7:00 a.m. and leave at 3:00 p.m. each day. "Impossible," he said. "I don't get in until 9:15 a.m. How will I know if you're working early in the morning?"

"His reaction astounded me because my office is on the 5th floor of the building and his is on the 11th," she said. "We rarely see each other except at scheduled meetings. So much for monitoring a person's work!"

Truth is, performance is never measured by "just being there," even for people who work regular business schedules. Receptionists, for example, who are expected to be at a specific location during business hours are not evaluated on their presence alone. They are measured and valued on the quality of their service (how pleasant and helpful they are to visitors and employees), the timeliness of the service (how soon after a visitor arrives do they greet the person and offer assistance), their response in critical situations (how they handle unwanted or dangerous intruders), and so on.

Exercise—Understanding Your Own Communications

To help understand your own management style, log your interactions with your employees for one week: who you met with and for how long; who you spoke to over the phone and for how long; who you e-mailed, memoed, and so on. At the end of the week assess how much face-to-face interaction you really have with your staff. Probably not as much as you thought.

Issues of Trust

J. Kermit Campbell, the former CEO of Herman Miller, Inc., a Fortune 500 manufacturer of office furniture, thinks you must liberate the human spirit as a way to improve organizational performance.

> Have you ever stood in a swimming pool and caught a leaping four-year old? The first time, you see the hesitation, fear, and excitement on the child's face. After the first leap, you can't stop the youngster from climbing out and leaping in again and again.
>
> In a nutshell, that's my idea of leadership, but it may surprise you that the leader in my metaphor isn't the adult. It's the child. Managers today are leaping into waters of risk, constant change, and increasingly tougher competition—and it's scary.
>
> So who's the grown-up on the scene? Who's there to catch us when we leap into the uncertainty of business conditions? The answer is, the people in our organizations. The creativity and commitment of our employees, the skills and knowledge of a diverse organization, the accumulated

wisdom of our past experiences—all this is what will catch us. What we as leaders have to do is, like the child on the edge of the pool, trust in our people.

—Excerpt reprinted from Healthy Companies
—*Leadership for the New Workplace*[1]

Building Trust

If you're going to jump into the alternative work arrangement waters, you want to feel that there's a high level of trust between you and the employee—trust that has been built up over time. In the case of new hires who immediately go on alternative work arrangements, which is occasionally done as a way of attracting new talent, you're asked to take a leap of faith. Even though you have adequate ways of measuring the performance of someone moving into an alternative work arrangement, it is still a bit unnerving. It's important that you and the employee have a history of honest communication and confidence about meeting expectations. That way, for example, when a telecommuter calls in and says he's been sick in the morning, but has been at his computer all afternoon, you won't experience any doubt when you log your records as "$\frac{1}{2}$ day sick."

Trust works both ways. Employees must feel confident that you believe in and stand behind the alternative work arrangement. That means you have realistic expectations about the arrangement; that you don't expect it to be free of problems in its early stages. It also means that unless there is a business reason to end the arrangement, you're prepared to work with an employee to solve problems creatively.

---

[1] *Healthy Companies—Leadership in the New Workplace* (Vol. 4, Jan. 1994), newsletter published by Healthy Companies, a nonprofit Washington, D.C.-based organization promoting a new vision of organizational health as the key to America's social and economic health.

Benchmarks of your trust in the employee include:

- Having a positive attitude about the arrangement.

- Encouraging open communication of what's happening in the company and in the department and of issues and challenges of the alternative work arrangement as it progresses.

- Making certain the employee knows what he or she is to do and is accountable for performance.

- Keeping the employee eligible for the same promotion opportunities and salary increases as people working on a regular schedule.

Defining Objectives

Together, you and the employee need to set *objectives,* or desired outcomes, for the job that are both realistic and measurable. Use time frames, quality standards, and other tools to measure success.

When setting objectives, keep three questions in mind.

1. What does this job need to accomplish?

2. By when must the job be accomplished?

3. How will we be able to evaluate whether the objective has been accomplished effectively?

What's an Objective? What's a Standard?

Objective: *Solve and correct problems found during the testing stage of new software products within two months of such problems being uncovered.*

Standard: Written report to management within 10 days of the problem being pinpointed. When problem has been solved, the software must be tested again and the average client satisfaction rating should be "exceeds expectations" based on a scale of 1–5.

Objective: *Identify a new plant location within 50 miles of the present location by December of this year.*

Standard: Develop a list of sites that meet our criteria by April 1, visit all potential sites with senior managers by August 1; pare down the list to two sites by September 1; present to board directors a preliminary report by October 1; arrange site visit of both sites for executive board members and have a complete report to board with final recommendations by November 1.

Objective: *Design and conduct a mandatory program that will train managers in how to respond to workplace violence by October 31.*

Standard: Design to be completed by June. Communication of program should be manger-wide and attendance at training sessions should be 95 percent or better. Training programs to be conducted and completed by October 31. Average manager evaluation should be "extremely useful." Follow-up training recommendations due December 1.

As a manager you might assume that all employees understand what is expected of them and how their work contributes to the overall success of the company and their division or department. Yet according to research, even employees on regular schedules are unclear as to why they do about one-third of their jobs. And unless a person understands how each part of the job fits into the broader picture, chances are he or she will think it unimportant and do it in a less than professional manner or not do it at all.

Employees on alternative work arrangements can feel even more disassociated from the company's goals, especially if they work off site. So make certain that each time you talk about objectives, the employee understands how particular tasks relate to the company and the department.

Monitoring Performance

When you're instituting an alternative work arrangement, nothing is more important than ongoing monitoring to enhance the arrangement and prevent irritations and stumbling blocks from becoming problems. Managers who supervise people working closely with the public via the phones (for example, people handling reservations, taking orders or fielding complaints) are already accustomed to using voice digital recorders to oversee the quality of the phone interaction. The same approach can be used with telecommuters. In the early stages of any alternative work arrangement you might want weekly feedback/coaching/brainstorming meetings. When all parties feel comfortable with the arrangement, time between meetings can be lengthened.

Feedback

An important element when monitoring an alternative work arrangement is to provide ongoing and useful feedback. Giving information about how one person's actions affects others tends to work like a guided missile system: It helps people stay "on target." Here are some criteria for useful feedback, developed by The N.T.L. Institute for Applied Behavioral Science.

▶ It's descriptive rather than evaluative. "The report you handed in yesterday didn't take into consideration the new policy decision we announced at the last staff meeting. I am concerned because of the lack of information or misunderstanding you have of the meetings—formal and informal—that you're not attending because of your flextime schedule." By describing one's own reaction, you reduce someone's need to react defensively.

▶ It is specific rather than general. To be told that one is "inefficient" will probably not be useful as to be told that "Just last week I asked you to include in your report a section on what the competition was doing in this area. That information is not here. It's too late to hold up the report from being circulated, but I feel as if I am circulating an incomplete study.

▶ It is directed toward behavior which the receiver can do something about. If the receiver is not intellectually capable of filing the report or there is no way that he or she can find out what the competition is doing, then his or her frustration is only increased. Providing feedback to change shortcomings over which the person has no control would be inappropriate.

▶ It is well timed. In general, feedback is most useful at the earliest opportunity after the given behavior. "Yesterday, when you left early as per your new schedule, you didn't call Jack to get the supplies we needed. Because they weren't here, we assumed they weren't available and we didn't get out the work we should have."

▶ It is checked to ensure clear communication. One way of doing this is to have the receiver rephrase the feedback she or he has received to see if it corresponds to what the sender had in mind. "You're saying that because I forgot to order the toner and the disks we didn't get the bulletins out?"

Keep in mind that the reason for sharing the observations is to help the person who is receiving them, so provide feedback with an attitude of caring, not in a judgmental fashion. You're not saying this because you want to prove that you know better. You're doing it because you want behavior to change. Also, be selective. Choose those things that will be most helpful to the other person. Share *two* or *three critical points* that the receiver can build on. And don't forget that feedback should be balanced, which means you should also share observation which *support* and *encourage* the person you're talking to.

Getting Feedback from Colleagues

The purpose of asking coworkers for feedback on how a colleague's alternative work schedule is working for them is not to point fingers or attach blame if all is not going smoothly. And people must understand that. A manager must communicate to his or her employees that the process is meant to bring about positive change. Often a colleague's specific, selective, and balanced observations can lead to a suggestion for a new procedure which would be enormously beneficial to the department and the person on the flexible schedule.

There's an additional benefit of coworker feedback. You can monitor (and nip before it gets out of hand) colleagues' resistance to the alternative work arrangement.

Mid-Course Corrections

Sometimes the employee senses there's a problem arising from the flexible work arrangement. Sometimes it's you or someone else who calls it to your attention. After providing the employee with feedback, the two of you will decide upon a mid-course correction. Often that's done by brainstorming for solutions or by coaching the employee to solve the problem on his or her own.

Brainstorming

When brainstorming, be sure to phrase the problem in a way that will stimulate ideas—lots of them. "How can you make certain that important information doesn't languish on your desk when you're out of the office and working at home?" Then follow the traditional brainstorming paradigm.

Begin by both you and the employee talking aloud and writing down every solution (wild and crazy ones too) that you can think of as quickly as possible on an easel pad without expressing judgment. Often you inspire each other. Then carefully go over the ideas one by one, and find something useful in every idea on the list.

Take the useless parts and either improve on them or throw them away. Combine the useful parts in creative ways. Even if no usable idea emerges at the meeting, the stimulation will probably lead to new thoughts later.

Exercise: Brainstorming Ideas

Situation: *An employee who has shrunk his work week from five to four days (with a commensurate cut in pay) finds too many objectives on his plate. He can't handle all of them.*

Possible Mid-Course Corrections:

- *Reassess priorities so that you both know which are the most crucial tasks to be done and reassign low priority tasks.*

- *Select the tasks the employees likes and excels at and reassign the others.*

- *Select tasks that need to be done in the early part of the week and reassign those that need to be done on Friday.*

- *Hire a part-timer to work on Fridays.*

Situation: *A customer tells you that every time he wants to talk to his representative, he gets her voice mail saying she's gone for the day.*

Possible Mid-Course Corrections:

- *Respect the prearranged schedule; don't leave earlier. Check messages after coming back from even minor errands like visiting the restroom.*

- *Make certain the customer knows when the representative is in the office.*

- *The rep should tell the receptionist where she will be during the day and have all calls forwarded; call-forwarding is instituted on voice mail.*

- *The rep calls in at the end of the day to pick up calls and return them.*

- *Back up should be arranged.*

- *Cross-training for employees covering for one another should be provided.*

- *The back-up person should meet the customer.*

Situation: *The team that the telecommuter works with doesn't want to reschedule its Friday meetings to accommodate his schedule.*

Possible Mid-Course Corrections:

- *The telecommuter reschedules his work-at-home day. (In the early stages of telecommuting, colleagues are often suspicious that the telecommuter is using Mondays or Fridays to stretch weekend plans—not to work.)*

- *The group schedules several small meetings at appropriate times rather than one large meeting.*

- *The telecommuter can have a "buddy" who shares information from the meeting.*

- *A teleconferencing system is established so that the flexplace employee can join the meeting electronically.*

Coaching

Coaching means *not* solving the individual's problem but helping the person solve his or her own problems. Coaches manage through *questioning* rather than *dictating*. They ask insightful questions that probe and encourage people to think further or to think through the steps necessary to solve the problem. Managers who act as coaches ask these types of questions:

- What do you need to accomplish in the time that you're in the office?

- What alternative schedules might you also consider if this doesn't work for the company?

- What can you do to make the arrangement more efficient? What can I or the company do?

- Have you thought about how your colleagues will respond to your telecommuting?"

Effective coaches also focus more on success than on failure. They respect the individuals they're coaching by spending time with them. They emphasize their potential and the potential of the new arrangement, not its limitations.

How to Portray a Good Coaching Attitude		
	If I Disrespect You	**If I Respect You**
Validation	I give orders without explanation.	I take time to set the context for our work.
Inquiry	I construct elaborate theories to explain your behavior	I ask questions to understand you.
Possibility	I focus on short-term expectations.	I keep a long-term perspective.
Responsibility	I see "you" versus "me."	I become your committed partner.

—Marilyn J. Darling, President
of Signet Consulting Group in Boston

The real value of coaching lies down the road. It develops an employee's confidence and ability to think through challenges and work out solutions independently. You're not bombarded with an employee's "little" problems on a daily basis, and your time is freed up to concentrate on larger, more important matters.

Performance Evaluation

Because you have set up performance objectives at the beginning of an alternative work arrangement (and review and revise them regularly with employees), you already have the basis against which performance can be evaluated in an annual performance review. And once a person has seen the connection between the elements of his or her own job and the company's objectives, it's not difficult to establish a measurement and reward system that correlates a person's individual achievement with corporate objectives (wherever or whenever he or she works).

As in all performance reviews, look at the employee's contribution to the department's overall results and the level of consistency of that contribution.

Adding New Elements to Performance Evaluation

An employee's creative problem-solving ability is tested with the challenges inherent in alternative work arrangements. You, as the person's supervisor, have a concrete opportunity in the annual formal appraisal to comment on how a person handles the challenges involving communication, client contact, coworker sensitivity, flexibility to changing work flow demands, and the like.

In addition to developing plans for the upcoming year, allow time in the annual performance review for a discussion of the alternative work arrangement—how it's working, what can be improved, what the employee envisions as the future of this arrangement, if and how the performance is impacting on career development, and so on.

Consider the Performance, Not the Schedule

When granting raises, promotions and handing out plum assignments, don't make assumptions that the alternative work arrangement can't accommodate ambition.

Just because an employee works from home two days a week doesn't mean he or she wouldn't be interested in an assignment that would require three weeks in Japan. Ask.

Just because a person is working a flexible schedule and leaves the office at 3:30 p.m. doesn't mean that she wouldn't make an excellent manager. Managers and supervisors, as well as employees, can work flexible schedules very successfully. Presidents of companies have been doing it for years. (How many do you know who work a 9-to-5 day in the office?)

And just because a person isn't in the office whenever a client wants him doesn't mean he won't make an excellent partner. This argument has been shot down numerous times by accounting and legal firms across the country (and by other businesses engaged in service occupations). Think how seldom it is that you get the person you're looking for when you call a law or accounting firm, for example. They always have to call back!

Do Unto Others

The golden rule in alternative work arrangements is "Be as creative with scheduling with others as you would have others be with you." Once you've determined that the arrangement makes sense from a business standpoint, be ready to back up your belief with senior management, to advocate for your decision, and to ask for sufficient resources to handle work when an employee is on voluntary reduced time, on a permanent part-time schedule, or on leave.

And finally, keep in mind these tenets:

1. Apply the same standards and principles for granting and maintaining an alternative work arrangement to everyone—men and women, people from all cultures, managers and nonmanagers, working parents, and people without children.

2. Involve employees directly in working out the details for alternative work arrangements and for assuming more responsibility for their jobs. Remember: the more a person becomes a job "owner" rather than a job "holder," the more invested that person is in the outcome and the more productive.

3. Maintain a "can do" attitude. Encourage flexibility in thinking and problem-solving. You may have to refuse an alternative-work-arrangement request occasionally because it doesn't make business sense. But don't respond to an initial request by saying "no" immediately. Suggest another alternative. And don't scrap an arrangement just because you hit a snag. Fine-tune it on an ongoing basis to meet the company and the employee's changing needs.

?

No Easy Answers—No Right Answers

How would you handle these situations? Keep in mind some of the many factors to consider: the needs of your department, your corporate culture, how valuable the employee is to your organization, the morale of your department.

What Do You Think?

John comes to you asking for an alternative work arrangement, preferably a reduced workweek but he'll settle for two days of telecommuting a week. He's vague about how long he wants the schedule and offers no explanation as to why he wants it.

Do you ask why he's requesting this arrangement? If you do, and he refuses to say, would that make a difference in your response?

Someone tells you that he saw John filling out a medical insurance form and thinks that John's wife has cancer. Would you indicate to John that you hear there's some health problem in his family?

Assuming the John's wife has cancer, would that affect your expectations of John during this period?

At what point does talking about or asking about an employee's family become an intrusion on privacy?

What Do You Think?

You offer a promotion to Jasmine who is working on an alternative work arrangement. She asks if the new job will require her to revert back to a normal schedule. You tell her it will. She refuses the promotion.

How will you respond when another promotion comes up—one that Jasmine is extremely well suited for?

Would you respond any differently if Jasmine told you she and her husband were thinking of starting a family?

Would your decision be different if Jasmine were a man?

Chapter 10

Managing a Department on Alternative Work Arrangements

"I can handle one person on a flexible schedule. But if everyone in my department decided they wanted to work different hours or at home a few days a week, it would be chaotic," one manager said.

It would be, especially if you didn't have some experience and success with one or two people working alternative work arrangements and if you didn't ease into the experience gradually or have adequate systems and procedures in place. Assuming all that has been done, however, managing a diversely scheduled department can be exciting and enriching. It provides employees with the opportunity to take more responsibility for themselves and their jobs (a proven method to increase productivity), and provides you with experience in the arts of delegating, coaching, conflict resolution, team-building, and problem-solving—qualities you will find essential in the years to come.

Pilot, Don't Bail Out

Piloting arrangements for an agreed-upon period of time, say three months, doesn't mean you're going to bail out at the end of the pilot period. It simply means that during this time most of the kinks will emerge and that you'll be spending more energy than you might otherwise on the process.

Don't overwhelm yourself. Unless everyone in your department is going to be adopting the same alternative work arrangement, such as everyone going onto a compressed workweek, for example, start small. Begin with one alternative arrangement, and then add others gradually. *Staggering* the pilots gives you more time to focus on each arrangement's particular concerns and challenges and doesn't leave you feeling helpless and overwhelmed. Also, each pilot acts as an instructor for the next, enabling you to anticipate and solve challenges before they become problems.

Set realistic and measurable goals for the pilot. If, for example, you're piloting a telecommuting program with a group of five employees who work in the customer service department, you might want to have one or many of these or other goals:

- Make home office capabilities equal to on-site capabilities.

- Determine glitches in the technical performance of system and determine what is needed to eliminate them.

- Determine how telecommuters are responding to the home office alternative and what effect it is having on on-site employees.

- Identify other issues that would need to be addressed before making the decision on full implementation of the policy.

Continuity Issues

When people in the same department are working different arrangements, there is the possibility that work will be slowed down, deadlines will not be met, or that creativity will suffer. Consider these scenarios and their possible solutions:

Situation 1

The controller, working a flexible schedule, leaves the office at 3:30 p.m. each day. One of her assistants comes in at 10:30 a.m. each day and leaves at 7:30 p.m. and the other works from home on Tuesday and Friday. The erratic flow of information from one staff member to another makes it impossible for the controller to get financial reports to the president every Friday afternoon. What can be done?

The controller and her two assistants meet to determine how to work this out. Their brainstorming might result in any of the following:

- All parties prioritize work responsibilities so that the weekly report is at the top of the list.

- The telecommuter switches from Friday to Thursday in order to accommodate the need for full coverage on Friday.

- The telecommuter's input for the report would be on the controller's desk at the end of the day on Thursday.

- The assistant working on flextime comes in on a regular schedule on Friday.

- The president changes the day that the weekly report is due, since Friday was an arbitrary selection.

- The assistants learn more about each other's jobs, so that they can fill in for one another when the other is unavailable.

Other Solutions: _____

_____

_____

_____

Situation 2

The president of a midsized public relations firm is in the office from 8:00 a.m. to 6:00 p.m., but 6 out of his 10 account reps work from home three days a week—all different days. He is finding that creativity, his own and those of his colleagues, is being impaired. "We used to walk into each other's offices and talk through ideas. No one's around to do that any more," he complains.

Here are some possible solutions:

- One day is set aside when all the account reps are in the office. They get together over a long lunch to share ideas.

- Every morning the group has a telephone conference, during which they discuss some of their ideas and get each other's responses.

- The group begins an e-mail creativity pool. Instead of wandering into someone's office to talk about an idea, the person puts the idea out to her colleagues via e-mail. All group members check their e-mail creativity message box by noon and respond as quickly as possible after they've thought about the problem.

  Note: Collaborating by an *asynchronous computer conferencing system*—meaning that group members are never on-line at the same time, but leave messages for one another—has proved very positive. Unlike the situation when someone drops into a person's office and interrupts a train of thought, participants can absorb the information when they're relaxed, ready, and receptive. And the process forces group members to go on record with their differences. They just can't roll their eyes if they don't like something. They have to explain why.

Other Solutions: _____

_____

_____

_____

Situation 3

A benefits manager is working a reduced schedule and is not in the office on the day that a manager in the finance department calls with an important question that needs an immediate answer.

Here is how coverage can be maintained:

- The benefits manager has a beeper and has agreed that in case of an emergency situation, the office can beep her and she'll call in.

- Managers (and employees) are given guidelines as to what is an emergency request and what is an important request that can wait for an answer.

- The benefits manager and the compensation manager agree to learn more about each other's jobs, so that they can cover for each other in most instances. They use their own time to cross-train each other.

- After having been adequately trained, an assistant is given more responsibility in dealing with benefits concerns and, at the appropriate time, is adequately compensated for the additional responsibility.

Other Solutions: _____

_____

_____

_____

Client Expectations

Sometimes clients are the ones who object to the alternative work arrangement because they don't feel their needs are being adequately met. Because the loss of a client due to poor service can be damaging, even catastrophic, to a business, this concern ranks among the most immediate and urgent to managers and needs immediate response. Consider these scenarios and their possible solutions:

Situation 1

A client at a law firm objects to being represented by an attorney who is on a reduced schedule because each time the client calls the attorney, he has to wait for a return call.

Here are some suggestions to mitigate the client's concerns:

- The client should know the attorney's in-office schedule. If the attorney is on the phone, at a meeting, or in court at the time of the client's call, the attorney's secretary or assistant would be responsible for getting the message to the attorney ASAP.

- The client obviously respects and wants this attorney to handle his affairs. He could be asked what he would consider reasonable response time. The attorney and the client might discuss the definition of emergency, so that when the client claims he needs the attorney within the next two hours, he really does.

- A back-up attorney, familiar with the client's needs, would be on call if the main attorney was not there. The back-up attorney would be kept abreast of the circumstances of the client and sit in on most meetings the main attorney had with the client—at no additional cost to the client.

- The attorney could have a beeper number that the client could use when he needs help immediately.

Other Solutions: _____

_____

_____

_____

Situation 2

The customer service department of a mail order firm is staffed by four representatives divided into two compressed workweek teams. The first team works Monday through Thursday; the second from Tuesday through Friday. The company has begun to hear complaints from customers that the lines are always busy on Monday mornings.

Here is what can be done to satisfy customers:

- The company logs the number, length, and type of calls each day to determine when the greatest volume is. If, as it seems, the heaviest day is Monday, then the compressed workweek teams will both have to work on Mondays, with each group taking off one of the lighter days.

- If a holiday falls on Monday, both compressed workweek teams work regular hours the rest of the full week.

- If a holiday falls on Monday, both compressed workweek teams work 10 hours on Tuesday (to accommodate the high over-flow volume on Tuesday) and then each would work 6 hours on the next two lightest days.

Other Solutions: _____

_____

_____

_____

Situation 3

The public relations department at a New York publishing firm has three fulltime positions, all with similar functions—getting publicity for and promoting authors and their books. The three positions are staffed by a job-sharing team and two people on flexible schedules, both beginning at 8:00 a.m. and leaving at 4:00 p.m. The vice president of public relations finds that they are missing out on a few publicity opportunities because calls for last-minute author appearances are coming in from California after the staff has left for the day. Trying to set up these appearances, many of which are in California, when staff members arrive in the morning narrows the window of opportunity.

How would you expand the window of opportunity?

- One of the staffers comes in at midday and works until 9:00 p.m.

- If this is a problem for all the staffers, let them come up with a system of rotation that would be fair for all of them.

- One is responsible for checking the office phones every hour on the hour after 5:30 p.m. each day. If anything comes in that needs immediate assistance, that person would be responsible for handling it—either from home or by going back to the office. This assignment could be rotated.

- All the staffers need more familiarity with each other's authors, titles, and contacts, so they can cover for one another seamlessly. Regular working sessions to share this information are set up.

Other Solutions: _____

_____

_____

_____

Communication Difficulties

The amount of face-to-face communication that takes place in any organization is much less than one would imagine. But when alternative work arrangements are being used and people aren't working the same hours or in the same location, there's a greater chance that important information will be miscommunicated or not communicated at all. Since communication is the oil which keeps an organization running smoothly, it's essential that it be frequent, accurate, and in a variety of forms. Consider these scenarios and their possible solutions:

Situation 1

With so many people on alternative work arrangements, it's difficult to get together for staff meetings.

Which of these suggestions do you prefer?

- Have one core time when all employees must be present (for instance, Thursday from 10:00 a.m. to 2:00 p.m.). Hold luncheon meetings where everyone brings their own sandwich (or spring for an occasional "on the company" pizza lunch).

- Schedule several small meetings at appropriate times rather than one large meeting.

- Implement a buddy system between coworkers to share information . . . and then alternate meeting times so that no one person is always absent.

- Make certain all employees receive all interoffice communication, written or through e-mail.

- Post announcements in a prominent place.

- Have conference calls and e-mail conferencing as occasional alternatives to face-to-face meetings.

Other Solutions: _____

_____

_____

_____

Situation 2

Telecommuters are getting information from departmental meetings they're attending, but they are telling you that they feel isolated. One says he was astounded to learn just yesterday that the vice president had been fired for embezzlement three months before. They say they feel out of the loop and are afraid that people are forgetting about them.

Bring your employees back into the grapevine:

- Respond to the e-mail grapevine, where appropriate, to clear up misinformation ("Rumors to the contrary notwithstanding, I was told the loss this quarter is much less than projected"), to get out company information ("Just heard that the new marketing vice president is Alaine Alvarez"), or to provide your own personal info ("Yes, I'm exhausted. Our second child doesn't know day from night—yet. And I'm not sure my wife and I do either!").

- Make certain telecommuters are given the same "visibility" as those working from the office. Have them featured in the company newsletter; ask them to make presentations at meetings and conferences.

Other Solutions: _____

_____

_____

_____

Situation 3

Other managers are baffled by the number of people you have on alternative work arrangements. They are always wondering where a particular person is on a particular day.

Ease their misgivings:

- Make certain that everyone on an alternative work arrangement has circulated his or her schedule in writing to everyone with "a need to know" and that the schedule is adhered to. If changes are made, the changes too have to be communicated in writing.

- Make certain that people on alternative work arrangements leave voice mail messages that reflect their schedules and provide information as to how the caller can be helped in their absence.

- Have a master calendar created for everyone in your department to reflect everyone's whereabouts. That eliminates someone from your department saying, "I'm not sure of her schedule these days."

- Have those on alternative work arrangements create a script for receptionists or others who will be answering questions on their whereabouts.

Other Solutions: _____

_____

_____

_____

Co-Worker Perceptions

Despite valiant attempts to be "fair" managers occasionally find themselves caught between dueling factions: in-office workers vs. telecommuters, flextimers vs. 9-to-5ers, working parents vs. child-free employees. Sometimes these develop as a result of an alternative work arrangement. It's important to keep in mind that most people don't mind working extra hours or handling someone else's responsibilities for a few hours—occasionally. They become resentful if such a thing becomes expected, when they aren't acknowledged for their participation or contribution, or when they themselves aren't given access to an alternative work arrangement. It's important for a manager to monitor attitudes, both informally and formally, to prevent additional work from falling onto the shoulders of folks working regular schedules. Redesign of work is fine; overwork is not. They must create a team-oriented environment that's inclusive of everyone in the department and make alternative work arrangements available to everyone who meets the company's performance and tenure requirements. (As we have said before, all jobs cannot accommodate all alternative work arrangements. But it is rare that a job cannot accommodate *any* such arrangement.)

Consider these scenarios of perceived or real inequity and their possible solutions:

Situation 1

As a manager you recognize the additional pressures parents have and you are willing to accommodate people who want to be home when their children arrive from school by giving them the early flextime shift. To maintain adequate coverage in the department, you cannot have any more people leaving early in the afternoon. A man without children says he wants to begin the day at 6:00 a.m., so that he can leave by 3:00 p.m., at least for the next three months.

How could you handle this?

- Ask those on the early flextime shift if any would be willing to switch. It may be that someone no longer needs this arrangement, but hasn't thought about switching to a different one.

- Ask if anyone would be willing to rotate every three or six months. It might be that some would be willing to rotate, especially for the summer. And that might be when the man wants to leave early to get in nine holes of golf.

- Work with the person to figure out another work arrangement that would accomplish the same objective (getting off at 3 p.m. for the next three months). Would telecommuting a few days a week work? He could start the day earlier simply because he wouldn't have a commute. Would a four-day compressed workweek be amenable?

Other Solutions: _____

_____

_____

_____

Situation 2

Because your company is expanding globally, some evening and weekend work will be necessary in your department.

How will you decide who's on what schedule?

- Call your staff together to discuss the situation and work out solutions. Once you've explained the company's needs, bow out.

- Oversee the operation so that people with the necessary skills are present to cover operations during the evenings and weekends and that you are not short of coverage during regular business hours either.

- Offer some incentives for the least desirable time slots, such as compensatory time or, in cases of nonexempt employees, overtime pay.

Other Solutions: _____

_____

_____

_____

Management Guidelines

By definition, flexibility means having a minimum number of constraints. What follows, is not a step-by-step formal set of procedures, but a collection of guidelines for managing a group of people on varying work arrangements.

Budgets Consider any additional expenses your department will incur as a result of alternative work arrangements. This could mean equipment purchases (for telecommuters, for example), training in managing alternative work arrangements, cross-training time and costs, or additional costs for benefits (if job sharers, for example, both get benefits). These up-front expenses will probably be offset later, but you still need to be aware of them.

Work Design Splitting a number of jobs into their respective functions paves the way for creative reshuffling of responsibilities and has the potential to meet employees' needs; to optimize employees' strengths, talents, and desires to develop in specific areas; and to meet the company's productivity standards. Think about this when you're baffled about how you can make alternative work scheduling serve a number of people in your department. Have employees collaborate in the work redesign. Encourage them to match themselves with existing jobs or propose new roles based on the best fit with their skills and interests and with needed contributions. To the extent that it's possible, implement the work redesign.

Help from Human Resources Involve the human resources department in your alternative work arrangements plans. Most of the time they have a better handle on what other companies have done successfully and where they have had problems. They also can help you with arrangements. When one of the members of your department comes to you to discuss job sharing, for example, you might not know anyone you could recommend for a partner. Because the people in human resources have a broad reach throughout the company, they might be able to locate a job-sharing partner for your employee.

Job Responsibility Give employees ample responsibility for managing themselves, communicating to their colleagues, and reporting results.

Employee Problem-Solving Encourage employee to solve their own problems surrounding alternative work arrangements. When employees understand the parameters of time and coverage, they can often design unusual, and extraordinary functional, arrangements among themselves. Once their designs are implemented, you can be fairly certain they will do all that needs to be done to make the arrangement successful and effective. An added benefit: Working together to solve alternative-work-arrangement problems increases their team-operating skills.

"Big Picture" Window Micromanagers work themselves into exhaustion if, under the guise of "doing a conscientious job," they expect subordinates to come to them for approval all the time. Even if you are obsessed with standards, you have to allow employees the daily responsibility of meeting those standards. They should feel comfortable coming to you for help on occasion (something overly supervised employees never do), but they shouldn't have to check in with you on every move. Your responsibility is to focus on the larger picture.

New Technology Become familiar with and take advantage of the technology available that can help facilitate alternative work arrangements. This includes: local area networks (LAN), electronic conferencing, e-mail, bulletin boards within company systems or on the information superhighway, fax pumps, "more than beeper" beepers, etc. You might not need any of these now, but at some point they might be useful.

Department Time   Make certain you have at least one (preferably several) times during the work week or month when everyone is in the office at the same time. People need to see their colleagues and interact with them personally. Hold activities to bring telecommuters together with on-site employees. Well-run meetings announced in advance are fine. Social events are just as fine, because at these the grapevine is allowed to function, enhancing communication.

Time Boundaries   Establish policies that respect time boundaries for everyone. For example, discourage phone calls or faxes to individuals' homes after hours and encourage as much notice as possible for upcoming meetings or times when alternative work arrangements must be modified (either to meet departmental responsibilities or an employee's personal schedule).

Pilot Arrangements   Pilot all alternative work arrangements and modify them whenever needed. Three months is suggested as the average pilot period.

Termination   Understand that you have the responsibility to terminate any alternative work arrangement that is not operating satisfactorily or is not in the best interests of the company. Assume that responsibility after you and the person involved have done everything possible to make it work.

Calendars   Develop a departmental calendar so that everyone in the department knows who is where . . . and when. Add to it phone, fax, and beeper numbers where people can be reached when not in the office.

Scripts   Develop a "script" which you and others in your department will use when talking about people on alternative work arrangements to clients, customers, and other people in the company. It should be honest. But it should also provide easy and immediate access to back-up assistance. Make certain that employees, too, have voice mail messages which are clear and provide the caller with immediate personal assistance.

Cross-training   Increase cross-training in the department so that when one employee is out of the office another can easily cover the absent employee's functions. Most people are eager to learn more and increase their skills.

Supervisor Support Provide supervisors who may be working for you with ample amounts of back-up support, either through management training done by an outside firm or through ongoing discussions groups using a written guide (such as this book) to work out the managerial problems they may confront.

Evaluation While it may be difficult to be precise about the effectiveness of alternative work arrangements, it is not impossible to measure. Among the data to obtain: employee productivity data, work team productivity data, department turnover rates, department absenteeism rates, and recruitment statistics. Keep in mind that alternative-work-arrangement evaluation is used as much (if not more) to enhance and improve the initiative than to justify it. Use it to find out what and how you can do better. "Hard data" is important when doing an evaluation, but don't forget the power and influence of qualitative data. A story of how your best employee stayed with the company and didn't take a job closer to home at one and a half times the salary because she was able to work out a telecommuting arrangement is at least as effective as any statistic. And it speaks to the bottom line: The arrangement saved the company money it would have spent recruiting and training.

A Window on How You're Doing Issue regular updates to people "looking in." Senior management, other managers, human resources—even the press—is interested in the concept of alternative work arrangements and want to know the challenges and some of the creative solutions you and your employees have come up with. Make certain credit is given to the employees who are making it work—those working these arrangements and those working regular schedules but who are part of the team that makes it successful.

Songs of Success Let others know of the achievements of your well-managed department by speaking about the arrangements at trade meetings or company-wide meetings. Be generous with your support of other managers who are starting on the same path. If you have a company newsletter, suggest the editor do a story on how people are achieving balance in their work and personal lives as a result of the alternative work arrangements. Suggest employees share their experiences with the community.

?

No Easy Answers—No Right Answers

How would you handle these situations? Keep in mind some of the many factors to consider: the needs of your department, your corporate culture, how valuable the employee is to your organization, the morale of your department.

What Do You Think?

Your company, a utilities company, has a policy of paying employees two hours' compensation if there's an emergency and they are called in to work during their off hours. What if the employees who were needed during this emergency were working from home on that particular day?

How would you handle compensatory pay if telecommuters were asked to come in to the office during the days they were scheduled to work at home?

What Do You Think?

A couple of your regularly scheduled employees are grumbling about the flextime schedule that several of their colleagues are on. They are stirring up resentment among others in the department.

To stave off major headaches, would you terminate the flextime arrangements?

What Do You Think?

You have a small department of three people. One person has been working a flexible schedule for the past year, starting the work day at 10:00 a.m. Now another person requests the same schedule. You know you can't fulfill the request because that would leave the department coverage too thin in the mornings.

Would you consider asking the first person to revert back to a regular schedule to accommodate the second person's request?

Would it make a difference to you if one of the people needed the flexible schedule to accommodate appointments for physical therapy? If the reason behind the request was to allow for more sleep?

Chapter 11

Why Me? Why Now? . . .
Managers of the Future

Ultimately, you might ask yourself: If managing people on alternative work arrangements is going to require refining management skills and if it might create challenges not experienced in the corporate world before this, why do it?

Let's answer this question with a question: Why did the Wharton School of the University of Pennsylvania (one of the premier business schools in the nation, whose ultimate mandate is the training of managers) recently write work-life issues into its required curriculum?

Work and life issues go hand in hand with the future of corporate growth. When you talk about someone working on an alternative arrangement, it's not that the person is sloughing off. He or she is probably giving the job 100 percent or more—but it's being done at a time or at a place which works better for the employee. And it has been proven to work more effectively for business as well.

Dr. Stewart Friedman, professor at Wharton and a prime mover in the work-life curriculum development, told the *New York Times* recently that business schools must prepare future managers for a globalized corporate future in which personal relationships, flexibility, and negotiating skills will be more important than the number-crunching skills many companies look for now. "Managers will have to be more people-oriented," he said.

Regardless of your company's "people strategy"—whether it's cost-based (everything is done for the bottom line), competency-based (you need skilled, competent people to be effective), or commitment-based (you can effectively use people at all stages of their life and career cycles), alternative work arrangements make sense. Any manager who can articulate the benefits and business case for alternative work arrangements, and who can manage employees working on such arrangements, will be well positioned for career advancement.

Reading: For Managers
and Those They Supervise

Newsletters and Booklets

The Working Families Newsletter published monthly by Working
Families, Inc., a New York consulting firm in the work-life arena, provides
employees with information, tips, and strategies for balancing work, family
and personal responsibilities. Its news-to-use format focuses on finding
more of what people lack most: time, money and energy. Single sub-
scription: $24. Bulk rates available. Working Families, Inc. 40 E. 21 St.,
Suite 5, New York, NY 10010. (212) 674–4420.

Telecommuting Review published monthly by Gil Gordon Associates,
a New Jersey consulting firm specializing in telecommuting. Includes,
among other things, case studies, new product and service information,
legal and regulatory developments, and international news. $157 annually.
Gil Gordon Associates, 10 Donner Court, Monmouth Junction, NJ
08852. (908) 329–2266

**The Conference Board's Research and Roundtable Reports
Dealing with Work-Family Issues** are published and sent quarterly
to member companies and sold to nonmember companies and organizations. In a very accessible format you get a combination of research
findings and practical insight from leaders in companies already
involved in alternative work arrangements—from job sharing to

telecommuting. To find out how to become a member and to get a complete list of the Conference Board's publications, call (212) 759–0900.

Books

Everything a Working Mother Needs to Know by Anne C. Wiesberg and Carol A. Buckler (Doubleday, 1994). Not only do the authors weave their own personal, legal (both are attorneys), and financial experiences and knowledge into a very readable, informative book (managers never had such a fast, easy-to-understand review course of employment practices), they pluck strategic, commonsense advice on alternative work arrangements and other work-life challenges from others.

My favorite: When one of the kids gets sick, the husband stays home the first day. The wife makes sure everyone at her office knows that her husband is home tending their sick child. This lends instant credibility to the situation because people assume that if her husband stayed home, the child must really be sick. Then, when the wife says she has to stay home the second day, no one questions her.

Breaking Out of 9 to 5 by Maria Laqueur and Donna Dickinson (Peterson's, 1994). An excellent primer for the employee who is thinking about breaking ground in a fairly traditional organization by asking for an alternative work arrangement. The book provides step-by-step help in writing a proposal that will persuade and makes clear the real responsibility of employees in flexible arrangements. Useful in helping managers develop ideas that will sway *their* bosses.

My favorite parts: Those that help employees strategize and size up their own leverage—which, they may be surprised, is considerable.

The Job/Family Challenge: Not for Women Only by Ellen Bravo (John Wiley, 1995). An excellent book for employees struggling with the work-family balance to help them understand their rights under the law and their responsibilities to their employees. Lots of down-to-earth advice and ideas for taming the struggle.

My favorite part: The chapter on the manager's role in handling family leave and flexible schedules. Scenarios help managers understand what level of performance they can expect, from new mothers returning from maternity leave to how cultural differences impact on managing people on alternative work arrangements.